– 50+ ADVENTURES –

BROOKELYNN LANDIS

All Scripture quotations, unless otherwise indicated, are taken from the Holy Bible, New International Version®, NIV®. Copyright ©1973, 1978, 1984, 2011 by Biblica, Inc.™ Used by permission of Zondervan. All rights reserved worldwide. www.zondervan.com. The "NIV" and "New International Version" are trademarks registered in the United States Patent and Trademark Office by Biblica, Inc.™

Scripture quotations marked NKJV are taken from the New King James Version®. Copyright © 1982 by Thomas Nelson. Used by permission. All rights reserved.

Scripture quotations marked ESV are from the ESV® Bible (The Holy Bible, English Standard Version®), copyright © 2001 by Crossway, a publishing ministry of Good News Publishers. Used by permission. All rights reserved.

Scripture quotations marked TPT are from The Passion Translation®. Copyright © 2017, 2018 by Passion & Fire Ministries, Inc. Used by permission. All rights reserved. ThePassionTranslation.com.

Scripture quotations marked CEV are from the Contemporary English Version Copyright © 1991, 1992, 1995 by American Bible Society. Used by Permission.

ISBN: 979-8-9854911-1-1

Editor – Christy Distler
Layout & Illustrations – Camby Designs

THIS BOOK BELONGS TO THE FEARLESS:

_____

(Write your name in big letters.)

TODAY'S DAY: _____

IF LOST, CONTACT: _____

*Note: If you find this journal, please flip to an adventure and do one before returning.

ENDORSEMENTS

"Activate Love is the perfect tool for new believers, seasoned Christians, young and old. As parents, we are so excited to start many adventures with our children, teaching them the simplicity of just loving God and loving people everywhere we go. Brookelynn is a young woman who has learned what it looks like to live her life beholding the Beloved and then living boldly, walking in love. We are beyond proud of her and expectant for lives to be marked by this book."

— WILLIAM & EMILY HINN
PASTORS OF RISEN NATION CHURCH

"Jesus said that there was something about becoming childlike that we all need. I have found in the church in general, and in my own life in specific, it is easy and way too common to think that just because we know something...we can repeat it...we can teach it ... that therefore we have achieved it. Yet, that is so far from the truth. Why not let Brookelynn take you on this 30-day journey into simplicity with Jesus? At first, you may think, This is so elementary. But as you go, you will realize that "purity and simplicity of devotion to Christ" is what you were created for... and your Creator is waiting!"

— TOM RUOTOLO
FOUNDER OF CITY QUAKE

"Activate Love is your opportunity to be a "doer of the Word" ... and not just one who has heard the Word of God. Brookelynn is a passionate follower of Jesus who wants to spread the fire of God's love through you. This can be the best 30 days of your life in a long time!"

— MICKEY ROBINSON
AUTHOR, SPEAKER, AND FIRE-STARTER LIKE BROOKELYNN

"Brookelynn Landis is a culture shifter in the most beautiful way. She is led by love and gifted with a spirit of compassion like I have never seen. I believe this book will ignite people to step out of their comfort zones and go on the great adventure with the Father in a new, fresh way! This will be a tool to light a movement and a fire to all who will read."

– MICHELLE BROGAN
FOUNDER OF DANCE REVOLUTION

"**Activate Love** takes the complication (and excuses) out of living faith out loud. Brookelynn is a young woman living and loving intentionally and she's on a mission to help others take daily steps to do the same. I'm inspired by her practical approach to faith and I know you will be too!"

– MISTY LOWN, BESTSELLING AUTHOR,
ONE SMALL YES: SMALL DECISIONS THAT LEAD TO BIG RESULTS

"New believers and veterans, this book is for everyone. I love the practical and creative application of day-to-day challenges to be the hands and feet of Jesus. If you feel like your walk with the Lord has grown stagnant, or if you don't know the first step to being a follower of Jesus, this book will put action to your faith."

– ANNA BYRD
SINGER, SONGWRITER, WORSHIP LEADER

"Brookelynn is first and foremost a true lover of Jesus. I met her when she was four years old. She came into my prophetic gesture class at a family camp in Montana. From there she went on to become a beautiful worshipper and dancer, teaching and leading others. Brookelynn's desire for you, her readers, is to go deeper into the presence of the Lord! **Activate Love** will inspire you to always draw near to our Savior. Enjoy the journey and the creativity in this sweet journal."

– BARBARA ROBINSON
CO-FOUNDER OF PROPHETIC DESTINY INT. AND CO-FOUNDER OF FAIR HAVENS RETREATS

"As a dad I've seen my girl go from a shy person who internalized most of the input that she took in every day, to a woman who seeks God and has amazing courage and compassion to do the will of God. She loves BIG. You can catch some of our Savior's passion and love by taking on some of her fun practical ideas that she has you engage in as you implement the pages of **Activate Love**."

– ANDY T. LEFEBRE
PASTOR AND PROUD DAD

DEDICATION.

I want to dedicate this book first to the One who has brought me out of fear and into a place of being brave. Jesus, I give you all the glory! I also want to dedicate this book to all the people who are not sure if they can do brave things. Believe me, with Jesus you can walk this courageous thing out. He is with you, and I believe in you.

THE ADVENTURE!

INTRODUCTION

You're invited to go on a <u>30-day adventure</u> that will rock your world if you let it. This adventure is about **JESUS.**

IT'S ABOUT KNOWING HIM AND MAKING HIM KNOWN TO THIS WORLD.

It's about taking the gospel to your family, your community, and your nation. This isn't like any adventure you've been on before.

It will challenge you, grow you, and call you to a life of **GREATER LOVE AND COMPASSION.**

As a believer, you are called to live a life different from the world. You are called to live a life of the supernatural. You see, we aren't meant to be stuck in the four walls of the church. We were created to be courageous lovers of God—and people—

<u>WHEREVER WE GO.</u>

ACTIVATE LOVE ADVENTURE JOURNAL

You may wonder, How can I walk in courageous love? We walk in love when we first **BEHOLD LOVE** Himself.

In this 30-day adventure, before you go love people, you'll first learn how to **LOVE HIM**. We cannot do anything without Jesus.

It's because of His presence that we overflow with His love. Then after spending time in His presence, we take that big step of **BEING BRAVE** and go love the people around us.

Some of you may be confident in talking with every person you come in contact with, and going up to random strangers might be easy. Others of you may feel like that's the scariest thing ever. Believe me, I wasn't always brave. I was a "that's the scariest thing ever" kind of girl.

I became **SUPER SHY** and insecure when I was about twelve years old. I would stay quiet in groups, and I didn't think my opinion mattered at all. The thought of being brave and sharing Jesus with people seemed impossible. I believed that lie for many years. Through encouragement and a constant stirring in my heart of a desire to step out, I'd finally had it. I said,

~~**ENOUGH WITH THAT LIE.**~~

I began to take small steps in doing brave things. Soon those **SMALL STEPS GOT BIGGER.**

I would feel the prompting of the Holy Spirit to go talk with someone or show them a radical act of kindness.

It would be so nerve-racking, but I found out that the more I said **YES** to the Holy Spirit prompting me, the more courage I would have for the next moment.

I'll be honest. I still get nervous sometimes, and I don't always know what to say. That's totally okay, because I found the Holy Spirit to be the best guide and comforter in those moments of feeling so uncomfortable.

No matter whether you feel shy or confident, He wants to take you on a WILD ADVENTURE!

You were made for this. I believe that as you take steps of being brave, you'll discover **MORE COURAGE**, and loving people will become so simple and natural. It might be scary at first, but you can do it. **HE IS WITH YOU!**

ACTIVATE LOVE ADVENTURE JOURNAL

This 30-day adventure is not so that you can fill in the "I did something for Jesus" checkbox.

It's to **EMPOWER AND ACTIVATE YOU** to love Jesus with all your heart and to overflow with that love to the world around you.

In this book, you'll start out every day in His presence. Then you'll flip to the fifty-plus adventures of loving people, and pick one or a few to go on that day.

You get to have fun and be creative! This adventure is not for you to take alone; be sure to invite the Holy Spirit to join you.

Now is the time to **BE BRAVE.**
It's time to let the **FEAR OF MAN DIE** and allow the **LOVE OF JESUS** to consume you.

FLIP WHEN YOU'RE READY FOR THE ADVENTURE... →

HOW TO USE THIS BOOK

THIS BOOK HAS FIVE SIMPLE STEPS.

1. LOVE HIM.
Take time daily in the presence of Jesus.

2. LOVE THEM.
Flip to the adventures section.
Pick one, two, or more to do that day.

3. SHARE YOUR ADVENTURE MOMENT.
Go to your journal and write out what happened.

4. WHEN YOU FINISH THE 30 DAYS,
flip to the overflow part of the book. Discover ways to continue the lifestyle of love.

5. TAKE A FRIEND ON THE ADVENTURE.
Share your journey and encourage someone else to step out in brave ways.

ACTIVATE LOVE ADVENTURE JOURNAL

THIS JOURNAL IS FOR YOU AND THE LORD. YOU GET TO BE CREATIVE WITH EVERY PAGE. YOU CAN WRITE DOWN YOUR THOUGHTS, AND YOU CAN MAKE THINGS BRIGHT WITH COLOR, TEAR PAGES OUT, OR GIVE PAGES AWAY.

YOU HAVE FREEDOM!

TIME TO BE BRAVE.

ACTIVATE LOVE ADVENTURE JOURNAL

MY PRAYER...

Is that you will open this book and find every page to be an invitation to go deeper in your relationship with Jesus. I pray you would allow the Holy Spirit to be your guide in every moment. I pray that your eyes and ears will be wide open to see and hear what the Lord is doing and saying around you. I pray you would say no to fear and walk in courage. I pray for a fresh fire to come upon you. I pray for moments with people that are life-changing. I pray that your desire will be to know Jesus and to love Him with all your heart, soul, and strength.

WHAT DO YOU WANT TO SEE HAPPEN ON THIS ADVENTURE?

Fill this page with your thoughts and a prayer for the adventure.

ACTIVATE LOVE ADVENTURE JOURNAL

ACTIVATE LOVE ADVENTURE JOURNAL

THE GREATEST ADVENTURE!
A 30-DAY ADVENTURE IN THE PRESENCE OF JESUS

Our number one calling in life is to love Jesus and seek Him wholeheartedly. He loves you so much and wants to take you on an adventure in who He is and who He's called you to be. I believe that as you journey through this journal, God is going to mark your life in massive ways. I dare you to dive in so deep that you find yourself miles away from shore. Your daily yes to His presence will be vital for this adventure. Take these thirty days to lean in to Him and get caught up in His love for you. I believe that as you discover how much He loves you, any fear of loving people will fade away.

GET READY FOR AN AMAZING ADVENTURE!

THE BEST EXAMPLE OF LOVE IS JESUS.

JOURNAL IT.

Spending time in the presence of Jesus is the best adventure. Nothing compares to Him. In His presence we're transformed and He shows us so many glorious things. You'll want to look back and remember all that He said, all that He brought to life in the pages of His Word, and the prayers that He answered. This journal is for you and the Lord. You get to document the things He shows you and does through you. You get to be creative with every page.

ENCOURAGEMENT.

The devotions are created to inspire, equip, and activate what God has already placed inside you. I know that doing something brave can be really difficult sometimes, and that encouragement can be so instrumental in your adventure. You have the freedom to read the devotion that comes about on that specific day, or read any one that the Holy Spirit guides you to. Each devotion is created to take you deeper in Him and to encourage you to step out in courage daily. I believe in you!

ADVENTURE MOMENTS.

After you spend time with Jesus, you have the opportunity to flip to the adventures and pick one (or more than one). I believe God will grow you, challenge you, mold you, and do incredible things as you go on your adventures. This part of the book will be a place where you get to share about what Jesus did and what you learned through it. It's always amazing when we can look back on the adventure moments and be reminded of the goodness of Jesus.

WHERE DO I START?

If this is a new concept for you, if finding the time has been a challenge, or if you're simply longing for a fresh revelation, here are a few things I find to be helpful in the adventure of loving Him...

THE FIRST STEP IS YOUR YES!

It starts with your yes. Your choosing to say yes to spending time with Him every day is the first step. It's not always easy to sit in the stillness, but I believe your daily yes will create a wonderful rhythm as you pursue Jesus.

FIND A TIME IN YOUR DAY TO DEDICATE TO HIM.

The time you choose to spend with Jesus might look different every day, or you might decide that a specific time works best. I want you to look at your week and decide when you are going to set aside time to be in His presence. I've found that if I mark this time on my calendar or set a daily alarm on my phone, it helps me remember.

FIND A PLACE TO BE WITH HIM.

Matthew 6:6 talks about going to your inner closet to pray. A quiet bedroom or closet is an excellent place to spend time with Jesus. I believe this verse is speaking of a closet because it's a quiet place, no one is around, and distractions are very limited. You can always spend time with Jesus in your room, the park, your car, on a walk, or anywhere you can be with Him without being distracted by a thousand things.

WHAT SHOULD I DO WHEN I GET DISTRACTED?

It can be so easy to get distracted (I've been there). If possible, silence all possible distractions before spending time with Jesus.

POSSIBLE DISTRACTIONS:

- Phone
- Computer
- Thoughts about the day
- _____
- _____
- _____

If you feel the need to check your phone or think long on something that doesn't matter in the moment, say no to that distraction and fix your eyes on Him again. Your time together will be so much sweeter if you can give your undivided attention to Him.

SIMPLY LOVE HIM.

You've come to a secret place to be with Him, and you've silenced distractions. Now what? Above all, Jesus delights in your just being with Him. You don't have to strive in His presence or try to check off as much as you can in your Bible reading. This adventure isn't about that; it's simply about loving Him.

[**THIS IS NOT RELIGION, BUT FRIENDSHIP. IT'S NOT OUT OF OBLIGATION, BUT OUT OF HUNGER.**]

IN WHAT WAYS CAN YOU LOVE HIM?

You can love Jesus in many ways. Here are some ideas for what you can do as you spend time in His presence:

▶ **WELCOME HIM.**
When you invite and welcome the Lord, it's your becoming aware of His presence around you and your saying that you don't want to only read about Him. You desire for the author to be present in every moment with you. He wants to dwell with you!

▶ **EXALT HIM.**
Take time to lift up the name of Jesus and tell Him how wonderful He is.

▶ **PRAISE HIM.**
Praise is powerful. It's declaring how good He is. You can sing, shout, dance, kneel, clap, play an instrument, or lift up a spontaneous song before Him. This can happen in silence or along with your favorite worship playlist. (See Psalm 95:2.)

▶ **READ THE WORD.**
You can start off by asking the Holy Spirit to lead you to a passage in the Bible. Take your time reading the Scriptures. You don't want to rush through it, but to meditate on the Word. Ask the Holy Spirit questions as you read aloud, and when something moves you, then pause and search the meaning of what you are reading. He wants to speak to you through His Living Word. (See Hebrews 4:12.)

▶ **SHARE & LISTEN.**
Silence the noise in your mind and lean in to the Father. He wants to speak to you through His Spirit. You can ask Him something, listen to what He's saying, share what's on your heart, and go back and forth in conversation. He loves sharing His thoughts with His children. Write in your journal the things you feel in your heart, even if you're still learning to know His voice (it's a journey for everyone). Writing what you hear will help you grow, and what He spoke to you will be a glorious thing to look back on.

▶ **PRAYER.**
Prayer is a powerful weapon. You can pray in the Spirit, you can say your prayer aloud or in your mind, or you can write your prayer in the "Respond" area in your journal. (See Jeremiah 29:12 & Mark 11:24.)

*Prayer point ideas: Deeper revelation, friends, family, open doors, divine appointments, boldness, and a radical love for people.

▶ **REST IN HIS PRESENCE.**
This is simply sitting or lying down in the presence of Jesus and thinking about who He is. You can do this in silence or with music playing quietly. (Psalm 23:2-3.)

THIS JOURNEY IS NOT ABOUT COMPLETING SOME OR ALL OF THESE IDEAS. IT'S ABOUT CONNECTING WITH JESUS. IT'S ABOUT LOVING HIM AND LEANING BACK AGAINST HIS CHEST AND FEELING HIS HEARTBEAT FOR YOU.

DAY ONE

I look to you, Father. You're my greatest desire. I am so thankful for your presence. All my attention is toward you. I give you this space and this time. Let your Spirit come and fill this room today. Thank you for being my Shepherd and leading me. I'm available for you. Come move and have your way. Take me on an adventure in your love! Amen.

TODAY I'M THANKFUL FOR...

SCRIPTURE I'M READING...

HIGHLIGHTS FROM THE WORD...

What is the Holy Spirit highlighting to me in Scripture, and what's on His heart about it?

ACTIVATE LOVE ADVENTURE JOURNAL

HOW I'M GOING TO APPLY WHAT I READ TODAY TO MY LIFE...

Write it out boldly here!

"Speak, for your servant is listening." – 1 SAMUEL 3:10

LISTEN FOR HIS VOICE

Holy Spirit, what do you want to share with me today?

LEADING OF THE HOLY SPIRIT

Holy Spirit, what do you want to do through me today?

RESPOND

My prayer for today is...

Based on your prayer today, make a declaration about yourself or something you're believing for. Declare it here! Feel free to tear it out and tape it somewhere.

LET HIS FIRE BURN IN YOU AND HIS LIGHT SHINE THROUGH YOU.

ACTIVATE LOVE

I pray that you may be active in sharing your faith, so that you will have a full understanding of every good thing we have in Christ. — PHILEMON 1:6

Now is the time to awaken and **ACTIVATE LOVE**! To activate means to make something active, ready, engaging, functioning, or operative, so to **ACTIVATE LOVE** means that you're actively beholding the love of God and showing love to those around you. No matter whether this is a new concept for you, you've considered it but not pursued it, or you've been sharing the love of Jesus boldly for years, I believe that God is calling you to be a part of His army, and to rise up and be light in this dark world (see Isaiah 60:1). It starts with your willingness to say yes to **ACTIVATING LOVE**. We have the opportunity to shine for Jesus everywhere we go. Today is the day to say no to fear and to say yes to allowing love to be operative and overflowing in your life. He wants to use you in big ways!

BEHOLD LOVE

ACTIVATING LOVE starts with saying yes to knowing and beholding the One who is Love—God. When you know the abundant, deep, and outrageous love that God has for you, love will naturally pour out of you toward others. Loving people from that place is so pure. If you want to know how to love like this, or if you don't yet feel like you understand our heavenly Father's love, that's okay. He wants to take you on an adventure in discovering His love. Spend time in the presence of Jesus—through prayer, worship, and reading God's Word—and His love for you will become clear. God's love is an everlasting and never-failing love. When you come near to God, He will come near to you (James 4:8). He sees you and loves you deeply.

SHARE THE LOVE

When you've experienced God's love, loving people is easy. So simply stare and dare; take time to stare into the eyes of Jesus and then dare to love those around you. As you actively step out to love people, God will always meet you there. Your yes to **ACTIVATING LOVE** is the first step, and bravery will come as you continue to take more yes steps. Sharing the love of Jesus will become easier and easier.

When I was twenty-two years old, I felt the Lord leading me to gather a group together to go love people in Dallas, so my friend and I started a group with this mission. Whenever our group gathered, I encouraged people to step out, but I felt really nervous myself. I didn't know what I was doing; I just knew the Lord was with me and that He was calling me to do it. After gathering weekly to love people on the streets of Dallas, I realized that encounters of loving people weren't happening just once a week during our group outreach; they were happening daily in my life. Love started to overflow everywhere I went, and as I stepped out by loving strangers and friends, God would minister to those people so powerfully. Choosing bravery over fear is challenging, but God is with you. Keep stepping out. You can do it!

Your personality isn't something that should define you or stop you; Jesus is the One who defines us. We get to carry His love and share it with the world. The time is now. People don't have forever here on earth, so the opportunity you have to be the expression of Jesus's love wherever you are is so important. Your yes can make an eternal difference for someone. Be a part of the army of God. Your yes will take you on extraordinary adventures. Now is the time to **ACTIVATE LOVE!**

WHAT DOES IT
LOOK LIKE FOR
YOU TO ACTIVATE
LOVE TODAY?

*Now, go do it!

ADVENTURE

Flip to the adventures and ask the Holy Spirit what adventure He wants you to take today. After you take it, come back and fill this out. Have fun!

WHAT ADVENTURE DID YOU TAKE?

WHO DID JESUS ENCOUNTER?

Follow-up Info:

ACTIVATE LOVE ADVENTURE JOURNAL

THOUGHTS?

Fill this area with words/pictures from what happened and what you are learning.

DAY TWO

I look to you, Father. You're my greatest desire. I am so thankful for your presence. All my attention is toward you. I give you this space and this time. Let your Spirit come and fill this room today. Thank you for being my Shepherd and leading me. I'm available for you. Come move and have your way. Take me on an adventure in your love! Amen.

TODAY I'M THANKFUL FOR...

SCRIPTURE I'M READING...

HIGHLIGHTS FROM THE WORD...

What is the Holy Spirit highlighting to me in Scripture, and what's on His heart about it?

HOW I'M GOING TO APPLY WHAT I READ TODAY TO MY LIFE...
Write it out boldly here!

THE HOLY SPIRIT LOVES SPEAKING TO YOU. HE WANTS
TO REVEAL HIS MYSTERIES TO YOU TODAY.

LISTEN FOR HIS VOICE

Holy Spirit, what do you want to share with me today?

LEADING OF THE HOLY SPIRIT

Holy Spirit, what do you want to do through me today?

RESPOND

My prayer for today is...

▶ Based on your prayer today, make a declaration about yourself or something you're believing for. Declare it here! Feel free to tear it out and tape it somewhere. ▶

MY PRAYER POINTS FOR THIS WEEK:

1.

2.

3.

4.

5.

ACTIVATE LOVE ADVENTURE JOURNAL

ADVENTURE

Flip to the adventures and ask the Holy Spirit what adventure He wants you to take today. After you take it, come back and fill this out. Have fun!

WHAT ADVENTURE DID YOU TAKE?

WHO DID JESUS ENCOUNTER?

Follow-up Info:

THOUGHTS?

Fill this area with words/pictures from what happened and what you are learning.

DAY THREE

I look to you, Father. You're my greatest desire. I am so thankful for your presence. All my attention is toward you. I give you this space and this time. Let your Spirit come and fill this room today. Thank you for being my Shepherd and leading me. I'm available for you. Come move and have your way. Take me on an adventure in your love! Amen.

TODAY I'M THANKFUL FOR...

SCRIPTURE I'M READING...

HIGHLIGHTS FROM THE WORD...

What is the Holy Spirit highlighting to me in Scripture, and what's on His heart about it?

ACTIVATE LOVE ADVENTURE JOURNAL

HOW I'M GOING TO APPLY WHAT I READ TODAY TO MY LIFE...
Write it out boldly here!

"But the Helper, the Holy Spirit, whom the Father will send in My name, He will teach you all things, and bring to your remembrance all things that I said to you." — JOHN 14:26 NKJV

LISTEN FOR HIS VOICE

Holy Spirit, what do you want to share with me today?

LEADING OF THE HOLY SPIRIT

Holy Spirit, what do you want to do through me today?

ACTIVATE LOVE ADVENTURE JOURNAL

RESPOND
My prayer for today is...

Based on your prayer today, make a declaration about yourself or something you're believing for. Declare it here! Feel free to tear it out and tape it somewhere.

WHEN YOU KNOW
HOW MUCH
HE LOVES YOU,
THEN LOVING
YOURSELF AND
LOVING OTHERS
WILL BE EASY.

CHILD OF GOD

Because you are his sons, God sent the Spirit of his Son into our hearts, the Spirit who calls out, "Abba, Father." So you are no longer a slave, but God's child; and since you are his child, God has made you also an heir. - GALATIANS 4:6-7

You are loved and treasured! When you know who you are in Christ, you become a powerful weapon in the kingdom of God. Satan hates when a believer knows who they are in Christ and that the Holy Spirit lives within them. God made you for this time and this moment. He created you fearfully and wonderfully (Psalm 139:14), and you're the apple of His eye (Psalm 17:8).

WHO HE MADE YOU TO BE

When I was seventeen, I signed up for a beauty pageant. It sounded like a great idea, but I walked away from the first meeting and began to cry. I didn't feel prepared to answer the onslaught of questions that the judges might ask me about myself. I told my father that I didn't know how to answer these personality questions and that I had no idea who I was. My father sat me down and helped me remember stories about my childhood to discover who I was. When the pageant day came, I was nervous but able to step out in full confidence, knowing my identity.

Your heavenly Father wants to teach you and show you the wonder of who you are. It's okay if you have no idea. God wants to sit down with you today to reveal how He sees you. Take time to sit with Him; listen for His voice, read Scripture, and worship Him. You will discover the greatness of His love for you and the many good thoughts He has for you (see Psalm 139:17).

You're so important and valuable to Him. As you begin to see who you are and take joy in your unique qualities, you will take confidence in who God made you to be.

WHO HE IS INSIDE OF YOU

Not only can we walk in full confidence of who we are, but we can walk in the confidence of knowing that He lives in us. When we are a **CHILD OF GOD**, His home is in us. He's alive and He dwells within His sons and daughters. This reminds me of the movie **The Lion King**, when Simba looks into the water and sees his father's reflection within his own reflection. Then Rafiki points out that Simba's father lives in him. Rafiki's words are true for us too! The truth is, our heavenly Father lives in each one who has accepted Christ. We are children of the King. In the Father, we have freedom and can walk in bold confidence as His children. We are not slaves but sons and daughters (Galatians 4:7).

God is so much bigger than anything else in life. His opinions matter more than what people think. It doesn't matter what others think of you. Fear of what people think will steal your focus, but when you surrender that to God and walk in your identity as His child, then watch out world. He's alive in you! Get out of the man-made boxes, and let Him shine through you. Go on the adventures today as a child of God, knowing that your Father dwells in you.

ASK THE LORD HOW HE SEES YOU.

Write what He says here.

ADVENTURE

Flip to the adventures and ask the Holy Spirit what adventure He wants you to take today. After you take it, come back and fill this out. Have fun!

WHAT ADVENTURE DID YOU TAKE?

WHO DID JESUS ENCOUNTER?

Follow-up Info:

ACTIVATE LOVE ADVENTURE JOURNAL

THOUGHTS?

Fill this area with words/pictures from what happened and what you are learning.

DAY FOUR

I look to you, Father. You're my greatest desire. I am so thankful for your presence. All my attention is toward you. I give you this space and this time. Let your Spirit come and fill this room today. Thank you for being my Shepherd and leading me. I'm available for you. Come move and have your way. Take me on an adventure in your love! Amen.

TODAY I'M THANKFUL FOR...

SCRIPTURE I'M READING...

HIGHLIGHTS FROM THE WORD...

What is the Holy Spirit highlighting to me in Scripture, and what's on His heart about it?

ACTIVATE LOVE ADVENTURE JOURNAL

HOW I'M GOING TO APPLY WHAT I READ TODAY TO MY LIFE...
Write it out boldly here!

"Likewise the Spirit helps us in our weakness. For we do not know what to pray for as we ought, but the Spirit himself intercedes for us with groanings too deep for words. And he who searches hearts knows what is the mind of the Spirit, because the Spirit intercedes for the saints according to the will of God." – ROMANS 8:26-27 ESV

LISTEN FOR HIS VOICE

Holy Spirit, what do you want to share with me today?

LEADING OF THE HOLY SPIRIT

Holy Spirit, what do you want to do through me today?

RESPOND
My prayer for today is...

▶

Based on your prayer today, make a declaration about yourself or something you're believing for. Declare it here! Feel free to tear it out and tape it somewhere.

▶

TAKE THIS JOURNAL SOMEWHERE AND GET YOUR <u>BRIGHT</u> COLORS OUT.

Go watch the sunrise or sunset and draw what it looks like here...

ACTIVATE LOVE ADVENTURE JOURNAL

ADVENTURE

Flip to the adventures and ask the Holy Spirit what adventure He wants you to take today. After you take it, come back and fill this out. Have fun!

WHAT ADVENTURE DID YOU TAKE?

WHO DID JESUS ENCOUNTER?

Follow-up Info:

THOUGHTS?

Fill this area with words/pictures from what happened and what you are learning.

DAY FIVE

I look to you, Father. You're my greatest desire. I am so thankful for your presence. All my attention is toward you. I give you this space and this time. Let your Spirit come and fill this room today. Thank you for being my shepherd and leading me. I'm available for you. Come move and have your way. Take me on an adventure in your love! Amen.

TODAY I'M THANKFUL FOR...

SCRIPTURE I'M READING...

HIGHLIGHTS FROM THE WORD...

What is the Holy Spirit highlighting to me in Scripture, and what's on His heart about it?

ACTIVATE LOVE ADVENTURE JOURNAL

HOW I'M GOING TO APPLY WHAT I READ TODAY TO MY LIFE...
Write it out boldly here!

Some of the ways we can hear Him speak to us is through dreams, visions, prompting, pictures, words of knowledge, in Scripture, in peace, and through a still small voice.

LISTEN FOR HIS VOICE

Holy Spirit, what do you want to share with me today?

LEADING OF THE HOLY SPIRIT

Holy Spirit, what do you want to do through me today?

RESPOND
My prayer for today is...

Based on your prayer today, make a declaration about yourself or something you're believing for. Declare it here! Feel free to tear it out and tape it somewhere.

IF YOU CONSTANTLY
LOOK FOR OTHER
PEOPLE'S APPROVAL,
YOU'LL BE DRIVEN
BY FEAR. BUT IF YOU
CHOOSE TO FOCUS ON
JESUS, FEAR WILL BE
DRIVEN OUT OF YOU.

CRUSH FEAR

For God has not given us a spirit of fear, but of power and of love and of a sound mind. – 2 TIMOTHY 1:7 NKJV

God is greater than our fear! Fear can be crippling, and it can stop us from stepping out. But we don't have to give in to the voice of fear or feel defeated by it. We have been given the authority to silence the enemy (Satan) and walk in courage. Jesus is so much greater than our fear.

FEAR OF MAN

Fear of looking foolish can cause us to stay silent. Ultimately, this is rooted in the fear of man. If you want to walk free from the fear of others, the key is to daily surrender that fear to Jesus; tell Him what you're feeling. At the end of the day, people aren't thinking about any awkward moment you think you might have had. What they will remember is that you went out of your way to show them love. If you constantly look for other people's approval, you'll be driven by fear, but if you choose to focus on Jesus, fear will be driven out of you. God is love, so give Him your fears and let His love fill you.

CRUSH FEAR

Fear was something I struggled with as a child and teenager. I felt so paralyzed by it. My fear manifested in different ways, primarily as fear of speaking and being vocal in group settings, and fear that plagued me with nightmares and night terrors. When I talked to my mom about it, she told me to take authority over my fear, and reminded me that fear is under my feet and that I don't have to be afraid because Jesus is greater than my fear (see 1 John 4:4). My mom then gave me a permanent marker and told me to write fear on the soles my sandals, and to remember that Satan is being crushed every time I take a step.

Doing that was a huge help for me. One night I had a dream about a giant monster. At first I was afraid, but then I thought, **Oh, wait a second. You're not a big monster. You're under my feet.** The monster in my dream shrunk small, and I crushed it. Soon after that, I took authority and refused to partner with fear. Those dreams didn't scare me anymore, and I stopped having them. We don't have to live with fear. The God that lives in us is greater than our fear, and He has given us authority over it.

The Bible says that Satan walks around like a roaring lion (1 Peter 5:8). But the devil isn't a lion at all; he just wants you to think that he's stronger than he really is. The real lion is Jesus—the Lion of Judah—and He dwells inside of you. Romans 16:20 tells us, "The God of peace will soon crush Satan under your feet." When the voice of fear tries to silence you, look at Jesus. Be bold, be fearless, and remember that He is within you and is greater than your fear. Crush fear as you go love people today!

WRITE ALL YOUR FEARS HERE.

Be honest. Share even the deepest/biggest ones.

Then take this page, rip it out, stomp on it, tear it up, and bury it in the trash can.

PERFECT LOVE DRIVES OUT FEAR.

1 JOHN 4:18

ACTIVATE LOVE ADVENTURE JOURNAL

READ THIS UPSIDE DOWN...

I AM FEARLESS!

ADVENTURE

Flip to the adventures and ask the Holy Spirit what adventure He wants you to take today. After you take it, come back and fill this out. Have fun!

WHAT ADVENTURE DID YOU TAKE?

WHO DID JESUS ENCOUNTER?

Follow-up Info:

ACTIVATE LOVE ADVENTURE JOURNAL

THOUGHTS?

Fill this area with words/pictures from what happened and what you are learning.

DAY SIX

I look to you, Father. You're my greatest desire. I am so thankful for your presence. All my attention is toward you. I give you this space and this time. Let your Spirit come and fill this room today. Thank you for being my Shepherd and leading me. I'm available for you. Come move and have your way. Take me on an adventure in your love! Amen.

TODAY I'M THANKFUL FOR...

SCRIPTURE I'M READING...

HIGHLIGHTS FROM THE WORD...

What is the Holy Spirit highlighting to me in Scripture, and what's on His heart about it?

HOW I'M GOING TO APPLY WHAT I READ TODAY TO MY LIFE...
Write it out boldly here!

YOU MAY HEAR HIM QUIETLY IN YOUR HEART, OR LOUDLY THROUGH YOUR DAY. LEAN IN AND LISTEN.

LISTEN FOR HIS VOICE

Holy Spirit, what do you want to share with me today?

LEADING OF THE HOLY SPIRIT

Holy Spirit, what do you want to do through me today?

ACTIVATE LOVE ADVENTURE JOURNAL

RESPOND

My prayer for today is...

Based on your prayer today, make a declaration about yourself or something you're believing for. Declare it here! Feel free to tear it out and tape it somewhere.

LIST YOUR TOP FIVE FAVORITE WORSHIP SONGS.

1.

2.

3.

4.

5.

*You can even make it your playlist for the week.

ACTIVATE LOVE ADVENTURE JOURNAL

ADVENTURE

Flip to the adventures and ask the Holy Spirit what adventure He wants you to take today. After you take it, come back and fill this out. Have fun!

WHAT ADVENTURE DID YOU TAKE?

WHO DID JESUS ENCOUNTER?

Follow-up Info:

THOUGHTS?

Fill this area with words/pictures from what happened and what you are learning.

DAY SEVEN

I look to you, Father. You're my greatest desire. I am so thankful for your presence. All my attention is toward you. I give you this space and this time. Let your Spirit come and fill this room today. Thank you for being my Shepherd and leading me. I'm available for you. Come move and have your way. Take me on an adventure in your love! Amen.

TODAY I'M THANKFUL FOR...

SCRIPTURE I'M READING...

HIGHLIGHTS FROM THE WORD...

What is the Holy Spirit highlighting to me in Scripture, and what's on His heart about it?

HOW I'M GOING TO APPLY WHAT I READ TODAY TO MY LIFE...
Write it out boldly here!

THE VOICE OF THE HOLY SPIRIT IS THE VOICE OF GOD AND WILL ALWAYS ALIGN WITH THE VOICE AND NATURE OF JESUS FOUND IN GOD'S WORD.

LISTEN FOR HIS VOICE

Holy Spirit, what do you want to share with me today?

LEADING OF THE HOLY SPIRIT

Holy Spirit, what do you want to do through me today?

RESPOND
My prayer for today is...

Based on your prayer today, make a declaration about yourself or something you're believing for. Declare it here! Feel free to tear it out and tape it somewhere.

YOUR STORY IS LIKE A KEY OF HOPE.

ACTIVATE LOVE ADVENTURE JOURNAL

COURAGE IN SHARING YOUR STORY

For we are his workmanship, created in Christ Jesus for good works, which God prepared beforehand, that we should walk in them. — EPHESIANS 2:10 ESV

Your story is important. You're one of a kind. God intricately created you and knows every part of you, and He takes great joy in His creation (see Psalm 139). You weren't an accident. Your life has purpose. No matter how difficult or how wonderful your life has been, you are here for a reason. The freedom you've found in Jesus is something to testify about. The way He rescued you from your own times of desperation and despair can speak powerfully to a person who feels hopeless. Your story is like a key of hope. People will see the love, grace, and freedom of Jesus when you share about what God has brought you through and out of.

WHY DO WE SHARE OUR STORY?

When I was a teenager, I didn't share my story often because I thought that since I grew up in a Christian home, my story wasn't exciting enough. That was a lie I believed. Actually, my story just looked different. All of our stories look different. My journey looked like God's love encountering me in my lowliness, insecurity, doubt, and self-hatred. He showed me that He cares deeply for me and that I'm never alone, and He came into my most broken places and filled them with His love.

Everyone has a story, and all stories are important. Maybe your story is that Jesus healed you, helped you walk in purity, or gave you strength to overcome something difficult. Or maybe it's how He helped you in that place of frustration, fear, or rebellion. Whatever it may be, your story is something that's worth sharing. As you share, it may be what unlocks the door to freedom for someone else. When people hear what God has done in your life, it may cause them to pursue that same grace and love.

HOW CAN YOU SHARE YOUR STORY?

You can share your story by telling others how you experienced God's precious grace and mercy. As I share, I like to go through this simple three-step process:

1. Share what your life was like before you knew Jesus.

2. Share the defining moment when Jesus became real to you.

3. Share what God has done in your life, and highlight the freedom, love, joy, and peace that Jesus has given you. Share how He has helped you overcome your past.

Scripture is clear: a huge celebration happens in heaven when one sinner repents. No matter what has happened in your past, the Bible says that all of heaven stops to rejoice when you made the decision to follow Christ (see Luke 15:7). Your story is something to celebrate! Your story is powerful, and it can encourage someone. Don't complicate it. Don't compare it. Be bold and share it.

WRITE YOUR STORY.

ADVENTURE

Flip to the adventures and ask the Holy Spirit what adventure He wants you to take today. After you take it, come back and fill this out. Have fun!

WHAT ADVENTURE DID YOU TAKE?

WHO DID JESUS ENCOUNTER?

Follow-up Info:

ACTIVATE LOVE ADVENTURE JOURNAL

THOUGHTS?

Fill this area with words/pictures from what happened and what you are learning.

DAY EIGHT

I look to you, Father. You're my greatest desire. I am so thankful for your presence. All my attention is toward you. I give you this space and this time. Let your Spirit come and fill this room today. Thank you for being my Shepherd and leading me. I'm available for you. Come move and have your way. Take me on an adventure in your love! Amen.

TODAY I'M THANKFUL FOR...

SCRIPTURE I'M READING...

HIGHLIGHTS FROM THE WORD...

What is the Holy Spirit highlighting to me in Scripture, and what's on His heart about it?

HOW I'M GOING TO APPLY WHAT I READ TODAY TO MY LIFE...
Write it out boldly here!

THE HOLY SPIRIT'S PRESENCE IS LIKE NOTHING ELSE WE'LL EVER ENCOUNTER. THROUGH HIM WE ARE CHANGED, HEALED, AND TRANSFORMED.

LISTEN FOR HIS VOICE

Holy Spirit, what do you want to share with me today?

LEADING OF THE HOLY SPIRIT

Holy Spirit, what do you want to do through me today?

RESPOND
My prayer for today is...

Based on your prayer today, make a declaration about yourself or something you're believing for. Declare it here! Feel free to tear it out and tape it somewhere.

IT'S NOT OUT OF OBLIGATION.

IT FLOWS FROM LOVE.

ACTIVATE LOVE ADVENTURE JOURNAL

WRITE A LETTER TO JESUS AND TELL HIM WHAT HE MEANS TO YOU...

DEAR JESUS,

JUST BECAUSE...

TRY PICKING UP THIS JOURNAL WITHOUT USING YOUR HANDS.

ACTIVATE LOVE ADVENTURE JOURNAL

ADVENTURE

Flip to the adventures and ask the Holy Spirit what adventure He wants you to take today. After you take it, come back and fill this out. Have fun!

WHAT ADVENTURE DID YOU TAKE?

WHO DID JESUS ENCOUNTER?

Follow-up Info: 💬

THOUGHTS?

Fill this area with words/pictures from what happened and what you are learning.

DAY NINE

I look to you, Father. You're my greatest desire. I am so thankful for your presence. All my attention is toward you. I give you this space and this time. Let your Spirit come and fill this room today. Thank you for being my shepherd and leading me. I'm available for you. Come move and have your way. Take me on an adventure in your love! Amen.

TODAY I'M THANKFUL FOR...

SCRIPTURE I'M READING...

HIGHLIGHTS FROM THE WORD...

What is the Holy Spirit highlighting to me in Scripture, and what's on His heart about it?

HOW I'M GOING TO APPLY WHAT I READ TODAY TO MY LIFE...
Write it out boldly here!

"Show me your ways, Lord, teach me your paths. Guide me in your truth and teach me, for you are God my Savior, and my hope is in you all day long." – PSALM 25:4-5

LISTEN FOR HIS VOICE

Holy Spirit, what do you want to share with me today?

LEADING OF THE HOLY SPIRIT

Holy Spirit, what do you want to do through me today?

RESPOND
My prayer for today is...

Based on your prayer today, make a declaration about yourself or something you're believing for. Declare it here! Feel free to tear it out and tape it somewhere.

WHEN YOU LIVE
COMPASSIONATELY,
YOU STOP STRIVING TO
PROVE SOMETHING TO
OTHERS BECAUSE YOU'RE
NOW AIMING TO BE LIKE
JESUS FOR SOMEONE.

ACTIVATE LOVE ADVENTURE JOURNAL

COMPASSION

Therefore, as God's chosen people, holy and dearly loved, clothe yourselves with compassion, kindness, humility, gentleness and patience. – COLOSSIANS 3:12

Jesus ministered to people because of His deep love and compassion for them. This led Him to heal the sick, raise the dead, and die on the cross for us. He saw people in need, and He was moved with compassion and He healed them. And when we have a personal relationship with Jesus, His compassion will fill us and overflow as we interact with other people.

CLOTHE YOURSELF WITH COMPASSION

As children of God, we are to clothe ourselves with compassion. Doing this is simply seeing people through eyes of love. It's seeing their needs and acting instead of ignoring those needs. Compassion is showing others that you care about them—smiling at a person who looks lonely, asking how someone is doing and listening intently to them, or praying for someone who is sick. It's sharing the love of Jesus—doing the things that He did—and it's doing each **Activate Love** adventure out of a place of love and not obligation.

Through our compassion for others, we find the desire to be courageous for Jesus. When we love people with compassion, we take our minds off ourselves and start seeing people from Jesus's perspective. Our thoughts then begin to shift from **What will they think?** or **God, please help me do this**, and turn to **Thank you, Jesus, that you love this person so much**. That compassion compels you to step out and love people more. When you live compassionately, you stop striving to prove something to others because you're now aiming to be like Jesus for someone.

HOW DO I WALK IN COMPASSION?

Walking in compassion is living with an open heart. It's choosing to see people from a place of love and not turning a blind eye or looking down on them. If you want to walk in compassion, then live with an intentional heart to love others — overflowing to those around you. I've gone through times when my compassion and desire to love people has diminished a bit. When this happens, I don't step out of my way to love people as much. In these times, I have to pray and ask God to give me His heart for people.

If you feel like you're lacking compassion, ask Jesus to give you more compassion for the world. Keep your eyes on Him. I believe that we become what we behold. When we behold our compassionate and loving Father, we look more and more like Him to the world. Don't focus so much on doing things for Him. Instead, rest in Him (through worship, prayer, and reading His Word) and let the overflow of your personal relationship with Him touch those around you. Jesus always made His Father His first priority. Search your heart and ask our heavenly Father to give you a greater love for people. He wants to clothe you with His compassion today!

WHAT DOES IT LOOK LIKE TO **CLOTHE** YOURSELF IN COMPASSION TODAY?

What does it look like to live more compassionately today than yesterday?

ADVENTURE

Flip to the adventures and ask the Holy Spirit what adventure He wants you to take today. After you take it, come back and fill this out. Have fun!

WHAT ADVENTURE DID YOU TAKE?

WHO DID JESUS ENCOUNTER?

Follow-up Info:

ACTIVATE LOVE ADVENTURE JOURNAL

THOUGHTS?

Fill this area with words/pictures from what happened and what you are learning.

DAY TEN

I look to you, Father. You're my greatest desire. I am so thankful for your presence. All my attention is toward you. I give you this space and this time. Let your Spirit come and fill this room today. Thank you for being my Shepherd and leading me. I'm available for you. Come move and have your way. Take me on an adventure in your love! Amen.

TODAY I'M THANKFUL FOR...

SCRIPTURE I'M READING...

HIGHLIGHTS FROM THE WORD...

What is the Holy Spirit highlighting to me in Scripture, and what's on His heart about it?

ACTIVATE LOVE ADVENTURE JOURNAL

HOW I'M GOING TO APPLY WHAT I READ TODAY TO MY LIFE...
Write it out boldly here!

> "Here I am! I stand at the door and knock. If anyone hears my voice and opens the door, I will come in and eat with that person, and they with me." – REVELATION 3:20

LISTEN FOR HIS VOICE

Holy Spirit, what do you want to share with me today?

LEADING OF THE HOLY SPIRIT

Holy Spirit, what do you want to do through me today?

RESPOND

My prayer for today is...

Based on your prayer today, make a declaration about yourself or something you're believing for. Declare it here! Feel free to tear it out and tape it somewhere.

PUT THREE {{ALARMS}} ON YOUR PHONE TODAY AND TAKE THAT TIME TO THANK THE LORD FOR HIS GOODNESS AND LOVE.

What times did you set the alarms?

ACTIVATE LOVE ADVENTURE JOURNAL

ADVENTURE

Flip to the adventures and ask the Holy Spirit what adventure He wants you to take today. After you take it, come back and fill this out. Have fun!

WHAT ADVENTURE DID YOU TAKE?

WHO DID JESUS ENCOUNTER?

Follow-up Info:

THOUGHTS?

Fill this area with words/pictures from what happened and what you are learning.

DAY ELEVEN

I look to you, Father. You're my greatest desire. I am so thankful for your presence. All my attention is toward you. I give you this space and this time. Let your Spirit come and fill this room today. Thank you for being my Shepherd and leading me. I'm available for you. Come move and have your way. Take me on an adventure in your love! Amen.

TODAY I'M THANKFUL FOR...

SCRIPTURE I'M READING...

HIGHLIGHTS FROM THE WORD...

What is the Holy Spirit highlighting to me in Scripture, and what's on His heart about it?

ACTIVATE LOVE ADVENTURE JOURNAL

HOW I'M GOING TO APPLY WHAT I READ TODAY TO MY LIFE...

Write it out boldly here!

LET THIS NOT JUST STAY ON PAPER, BUT LET HIS VOICE BE
WHAT YOU LONG TO HEAR THROUGHOUT YOUR DAY.

LISTEN FOR HIS VOICE

Holy Spirit, what do you want to share with me today?

LEADING OF THE HOLY SPIRIT

Holy Spirit, what do you want to do through me today?

RESPOND

My prayer for today is...

Based on your prayer today, make a declaration about yourself or something you're believing for. Declare it here! Feel free to tear it out and tape it somewhere.

I AM UNASHAMED OF THE GOSPEL.

ACTIVATE LOVE ADVENTURE JOURNAL

BOLDNESS IN SHARING HIS STORY

For I am not ashamed of the gospel of Christ, for it is the power of God to salvation for everyone who believes, for the Jew first and also for the Greek. — ROMANS 1:16 NKJV

The love of our Savior Jesus Christ is unimaginably deep. He loves us so much that He wrapped Himself in flesh and died on the cross for us. Jesus went through agony so that our hearts can be washed by His blood and our sins forgiven. He is the only way to eternal life (John 10:9). Our works cannot save us; only through the grace of Jesus can we be saved (Ephesians 2:8).

When someone repents and confesses that Jesus is Lord, they become a new creation (see 2 Corinthians 5:17). Giving your life to Christ means letting go of the old nature to follow Him. The most powerful thing we can do is tell others the good news of Jesus Christ. It is the greatest miracle and a free gift that we get to experience and share with others. We get to be a part of "HIS-STORY" when we share about Him with those around us. Seeing people come into the kingdom of God is the most exciting adventure we can be a part of. The harvest is ripe and ready (see Matthew 9:37-38).

WHY DO WE SHARE HIS STORY?

Jesus wants all people to know Him. His desire is for all to be with Him for eternity. Sadly, some people won't experience this because they will never know Him or they will reject Him by not believing that He died for them. As Christians, we are to not only follow His ways, but to also share with others that Jesus is the only way to heaven. In John 14:6, Jesus says, "I am the way and the truth and the life. No one comes to the Father except through me."

We have the opportunity to share with the world about Jesus. The gospel is the power of God, so we mustn't be ashamed of sharing it. God has called us to be free from shame and to take the baskets off our heads and declare His name (Matthew 5:14-16 NKJV). Sharing with someone about Jesus can change the destination of their eternity. That's the powerful reason why sharing Jesus is so important.

HOW DO I SHARE THE GOSPEL?

Sharing Jesus isn't complicated. It's simply telling someone about His amazing love and what He did for us. You don't have to recite everything perfectly or feel like you need to see someone make an immediate decision to follow Jesus. Just be yourself and invite the Holy Spirit to minister to the other person's heart. As you step out and share, the Holy Spirit will do the rest.

I'll be honest: my shaky confidence, and the belief that I lack the necessary knowledge, has stopped me from telling someone about Jesus. But I've discovered that Jesus didn't say, "Okay, be sure to share the gospel in this exact way." No, He just told His disciples to go and preach the gospel to all of creation (Mark 16:15). Sharing the gospel is showing people the love and power of Jesus Christ, and then inviting them to experience it themselves.

HERE ARE SOME TIPS THAT MAY HELP YOU AS YOU GROW IN SHARING THE GOSPEL WITH BOLDNESS:

1. Read the Gospels (the first four books of the New Testament: Matthew, Mark, Luke, and John). Read about what Jesus did for us on the cross, the story of His resurrection, what it looks like to follow Him, and the power of the Holy Spirit in the life of a believer.

2. Write out the gospel of Jesus in your own words. You don't have to make it long; keep it short and simple enough for people to understand.

3. Let the Holy Spirit lead you in your conversations. As you trust Him, He will give you the words to speak. You get to be you! Let the story of Jesus come alive in you and flow through you to others. You don't have to sound perfect. Simply share His love.

WRITE OUT THE GOSPEL.

How would you share it with someone?
Write your few-minute version here...

*WRITE IT OUT. PRACTICE IT. SHARE IT.

ACTIVATE LOVE ADVENTURE JOURNAL

STEP IN PAINT AND THEN PLACE A FOOT ON THIS PAGE. DO IT AS A DECLARATION THAT YOU'RE GOING TO BE ONE WHO DECLARES THE GOSPEL AND WALKS IT OUT IN BOLDNESS.

WARNING... THIS IS RADICAL

ADVENTURE

Flip to the adventures and ask the Holy Spirit what adventure He wants you to take today. After you take it, come back and fill this out. Have fun!

WHAT ADVENTURE DID YOU TAKE?

WHO DID JESUS ENCOUNTER?

Follow-up Info:

ACTIVATE LOVE ADVENTURE JOURNAL

THOUGHTS?

Fill this area with words/pictures from what happened and what you are learning.

DAY TWELVE

I look to you, Father. You're my greatest desire. I am so thankful for your presence. All my attention is toward you. I give you this space and this time. Let your Spirit come and fill this room today. Thank you for being my Shepherd and leading me. I'm available for you. Come move and have your way. Take me on an adventure in your love! Amen.

TODAY I'M THANKFUL FOR...

SCRIPTURE I'M READING...

HIGHLIGHTS FROM THE WORD...

What is the Holy Spirit highlighting to me in Scripture, and what's on His heart about it?

ACTIVATE LOVE ADVENTURE JOURNAL

HOW I'M GOING TO APPLY WHAT I READ TODAY TO MY LIFE...
Write it out boldly here!

LIKE ANY FRIEND, THE HOLY SPIRIT WANTS TO REVEAL SECRETS TO YOU AND SHARE THINGS THAT WILL BRING HEALING, INSIGHT, FREEDOM, AND REVELATION TO YOU AND TO THOSE YOU'RE MINISTERING TO.

LISTEN FOR HIS VOICE

Holy Spirit, what do you want to share with me today?

LEADING OF THE HOLY SPIRIT

Holy Spirit, what do you want to do through me today?

RESPOND
My prayer for today is...

Based on your prayer today, make a declaration about yourself or something you're believing for. Declare it here! Feel free to tear it out and tape it somewhere.

IN WHAT AREAS IN YOUR LIFE CAN YOU SEE GOD MOVING MIGHTILY?

Take a moment today to thank Jesus for these areas.

ACTIVATE LOVE ADVENTURE JOURNAL

ADVENTURE

Flip to the adventures and ask the Holy Spirit what adventure He wants you to take today. After you take it, come back and fill this out. Have fun!

WHAT ADVENTURE DID YOU TAKE?

WHO DID JESUS ENCOUNTER?

Follow-up Info:

THOUGHTS?

Fill this area with words/pictures from what happened and what you are learning.

DAY THIRTEEN

I look to you, Father. You're my greatest desire. I am so thankful for your presence. All my attention is toward you. I give you this space and this time. Let your Spirit come and fill this room today. Thank you for being my Shepherd and leading me. I'm available for you. Come move and have your way. Take me on an adventure in your love! Amen.

TODAY I'M THANKFUL FOR...

SCRIPTURE I'M READING...

HIGHLIGHTS FROM THE WORD...

What is the Holy Spirit highlighting to me in Scripture, and what's on His heart about it?

ACTIVATE LOVE ADVENTURE JOURNAL

HOW I'M GOING TO APPLY WHAT I READ TODAY TO MY LIFE...
Write it out boldly here!

"Today, if you hear his voice, do not harden your hearts." – HEBREWS 4:7

LISTEN FOR HIS VOICE

Holy Spirit, what do you want to share with me today?

LEADING OF THE HOLY SPIRIT

Holy Spirit, what do you want to do through me today?

RESPOND
My prayer for today is...

Based on your prayer today, make a declaration about yourself or something you're believing for. Declare it here! Feel free to tear it out and tape it somewhere.

LIFE WITH THE HOLY SPIRIT IS ALWAYS EXCITING.

ACTIVATE LOVE ADVENTURE JOURNAL

THE HOLY SPIRIT

"But you will receive power when the Holy Spirit comes on you; and you will be my witnesses in Jerusalem, and in all Judea and Samaria, and to the ends of the earth." – ACTS 1:8

The Holy Spirit is God's promise to us (see John 14:16). God is three in one: God the Father, Jesus the Son, and the Holy Spirit. The Holy Spirit is the presence of God in the life of a believer. With the Holy Spirit within us, we can have a personal relationship with Jesus and walk with power here on earth.

The Holy Spirit's presence is like nothing else we'll ever encounter. Through Him we are changed, healed, and transformed. When we accept Jesus into our hearts, we receive the Holy Spirit into our lives and are equipped to live our lives with power. We invite the Holy Spirit to empower us, lead us, and use us, and His presence in our lives guides us, speaking to our inmost being, bringing healthy conviction in our actions, directing our steps, and revealing the wisdom of God to us.

Life with the Holy Spirit is always exciting. If you're a follower of Christ, He has made His home in you. Now it's time to allow Him to move and flow through you. Each day, He wants to use you to minister and transform those around you.

THE POWER OF THE HOLY SPIRIT

When you ask Jesus to be your Lord and Savior, you invite the Holy Spirit to dwell within you. The Bible also speaks about a baptism of the Holy Spirit, which is the moment in your life when you invite the Holy Spirit to rest upon you and empower you to live a lifestyle of love and power (see Matthew 3:11). In Acts 2, the Holy Spirit came upon the 120 people in the Upper Room like a mighty rushing wind and rested upon them with what seemed to be tongues of fire. As we intentionally invite the Holy Spirit to empower us, we get to walk in the same signs, wonders, and miracles that the believers did in Acts.

The Holy Spirit enables us to boldly share our faith, and it is His power that works in us when we pray for the sick and see them healed, cast out demons, and raise the dead (see Matthew 10:8). The Holy Spirit wants to move through you in mighty ways. As you go throughout your day, yield your heart to what He's doing and be open to moments when the He wants to use you as His instrument to touch someone's life.

THE VOICE OF THE HOLY SPIRIT

The Holy Spirit dwells in those who believe in Jesus, and every one of us can hear from Him. How do we hear the voice of the Holy Spirit? We simply give Him our attention and listen. It's not a one-way conversation; first we listen to His voice, and then we respond.

Like any friend, the Holy Spirit wants to reveal secrets to you and share things that will bring healing, insight, freedom, and revelation to you and to those you're ministering to. The Holy Spirit speaks with power and authority. What He says will line up with Scripture, and His voice is never condemning or fear-instilling. He speaks life-giving truth. Think about Jesus in Scripture—His voice and His nature. The voice of the Holy Spirit is the voice of God and will always align with the voice and nature of Jesus found in God's Word.

The Holy Spirit can speak to us in different ways. He speaks through a sense of deep peace, dreams, visions, pictures in your mind, a whisper, or a "knowing" inside. He can also highlight specific passages of Scripture to you or provide a word of knowledge, which is simply a God-given awareness of a specific detail or circumstance that you would not have known otherwise. Today, ask the Holy Spirit to speak to you in one of these ways or in a way you haven't heard Him speak to you before. As you spend time daily with the Holy Spirit, you will get to know His voice better (see John 10:27). Lean in and listen! He loves talking with you.

HOLY SPIRIT POWER

Take time today to ask the Holy Spirit for a fresh baptism of His fire. Ask Him to come and invade your life with His power.

ACTIVATE LOVE ADVENTURE JOURNAL

"I PRAY THAT OUT OF HIS GLORIOUS RICHES HE MAY STRENGTHEN YOU WITH **POWER** THROUGH HIS SPIRIT IN YOUR INNER BEING, SO THAT CHRIST MAY DWELL IN YOUR HEARTS THROUGH FAITH. AND I PRAY THAT YOU, BEING ROOTED AND ESTABLISHED IN LOVE, MAY HAVE **POWER,** TOGETHER WITH ALL THE LORD'S HOLY PEOPLE, TO GRASP HOW WIDE AND LONG AND HIGH AND DEEP IS THE LOVE OF CHRIST, AND TO KNOW THIS LOVE THAT SURPASSES KNOWLEDGE—THAT YOU MAY BE FILLED TO THE MEASURE OF ALL THE FULLNESS OF GOD."

EPHESIANS 3:16-19

THE VOICE OF THE HOLY SPIRIT

What does it look like for you to lean in and hear Him?

ACTIVATE LOVE ADVENTURE JOURNAL

ADVENTURE

Flip to the adventures and ask the Holy Spirit what adventure He wants you to take today. After you take it, come back and fill this out. Have fun!

WHAT ADVENTURE DID YOU TAKE?

WHO DID JESUS ENCOUNTER?

Follow-up Info: 💬

THOUGHTS?

Fill this area with words/pictures from what happened and what you are learning.

DAY FOURTEEN

I look to you, Father. You're my greatest desire. I am so thankful for your presence. All my attention is toward you. I give you this space and this time. Let your Spirit come and fill this room today. Thank you for being my Shepherd and leading me. I'm available for you. Come move and have your way. Take me on an adventure in your love! Amen.

TODAY I'M THANKFUL FOR...

SCRIPTURE I'M READING...

HIGHLIGHTS FROM THE WORD...

What is the Holy Spirit highlighting to me in Scripture, and what's on His heart about it?

HOW I'M GOING TO APPLY WHAT I READ TODAY TO MY LIFE...
Write it out boldly here!

Be still, mind. Be still, heart.
Be still and listen.

LISTEN FOR HIS VOICE

Holy Spirit, what do you want to share with me today?

LEADING OF THE HOLY SPIRIT

Holy Spirit, what do you want to do through me today?

RESPOND

My prayer for today is...

Based on your prayer today, make a declaration about yourself or something you're believing for. Declare it here! Feel free to tear it out and tape it somewhere.

FOLD THE CORNER OF THIS PAGE.

Come back to it in a few months and check your life to see if His presence is still a priority.

ACTIVATE LOVE ADVENTURE JOURNAL

ADVENTURE

Flip to the adventures and ask the Holy Spirit what adventure He wants you to take today. After you take it, come back and fill this out. Have fun!

WHAT ADVENTURE DID YOU TAKE?

WHO DID JESUS ENCOUNTER?

Follow-up Info: 💬

THOUGHTS?

Fill this area with words/pictures from what happened and what you are learning.

DAY FIFTEEN

I look to you, Father. You're my greatest desire. I am so thankful for your presence. All my attention is toward you. I give you this space and this time. Let your Spirit come and fill this room today. Thank you for being my Shepherd and leading me. I'm available for you. Come move and have your way. Take me on an adventure in your love! Amen.

TODAY I'M THANKFUL FOR...

SCRIPTURE I'M READING...

HIGHLIGHTS FROM THE WORD...

What is the Holy Spirit highlighting to me in Scripture, and what's on His heart about it?

HOW I'M GOING TO APPLY WHAT I READ TODAY TO MY LIFE...
Write it out boldly here!

"When he has brought out all his own, he goes on ahead of them, and his sheep follow him because they know his voice."
— JOHN 10:4

LISTEN FOR HIS VOICE

Holy Spirit, what do you want to share with me today?

LEADING OF THE HOLY SPIRIT

Holy Spirit, what do you want to do through me today?

RESPOND

My prayer for today is...

Based on your prayer today, make a declaration about yourself or something you're believing for. Declare it here! Feel free to tear it out and tape it somewhere.

TAKE A **MEAL** TODAY TO FAST AND TO BE WITH JESUS.

ACTIVATE LOVE ADVENTURE JOURNAL

REST AND REMAIN

"Remain in me, as I also remain in you. No branch can bear fruit by itself; it must remain in the vine. Neither can you bear fruit unless you remain in me." – JOHN 15:4

Breathe and rest in Jesus. Some of us need to remind ourselves of this often. Resting and remaining in Him is spending time with Him daily. Doing life without Jesus is like going throughout the day without water. Jesus is the Living Water, and we need His presence every day. Without spending time with Him, we cannot be fruitful or overflow with His love to the world around us. Trying to become love without spending time with Love Himself will make us sound like "empty noise" (see 1 Corinthians 13:1). Our highest priority and greatest adventure is to know Jesus and abide in His presence daily.

REST AND REMAIN IN THE BEING

You were made for a relationship with the Father. Remaining in Him isn't a once-a-week thing. To remain means to abide, dwell, and wait upon. It's spending time with the Father and abiding in Him every day. It's taking time to sit in His presence and at His table. You were created to know your Creator and have a relationship with Him. Sit at His feet by spending time in the Word and in prayer, getting to know who He is. God delights in you and is proud of you. Make His presence your first priority during this **Activate Love** adventure. If you have to say no to some things in order to be able to sit with Jesus, it will be so worth the sacrifice.

REMAIN AND REST IN THE DOING

The key to living a life of courage that produces great fruit is abiding in Jesus. When we live from a place of remaining and resting, all that we do will be from that place too. You don't have to work to see results in your adventures of loving people; instead, as you go throughout your day, just lean in to Jesus and you'll find so much rest in that. Your adventures will soon become a natural lifestyle of your loving Him and overflowing with that love.

When dwelling in the presence of Jesus isn't our number one priority, we often feel exhausted, empty, and closed off to ministering to people. I've been there, and it's not a fun place to be. Loving starts to feel like an obligation. Never forget the main thing: Jesus loves spending time with you and wants to go along with you on your adventures of loving people. If you realize that you're getting caught up in the doing instead of the being, then just come back to sitting at His feet. Jesus isn't condemning; He's waiting for you with open arms. In His presence, you'll find peace, healing, and a sound mind, and you'll discover deeper mysteries. Turn down the noise today and let Him quiet you with His love. Be filled and then overflow!

WHAT DOES IT LOOK LIKE TO REST IN HIM?

LET'S WRITE A "TO BE" LIST INSTEAD OF A "~~TO DO.~~"

☐

☐

☐

☐

☐

FATHER,
REFRESH ME IN YOUR LOVE TODAY. SHOW ME WHAT IT LOOKS LIKE TO DAILY SIT AT YOUR FEET AND DWELL IN YOUR PRESENCE. FORGIVE ME FOR EVER SETTING ANYTHING ABOVE MY RELATIONSHIP WITH YOU. YOU'RE THE ONE THING I DESIRE AND SEEK AFTER. I TURN MY ATTENTION TO YOU TODAY, AND I INVITE YOU TO COME INVADE EVERYTHING I DO WITH YOUR PRESENCE. I LOVE YOU.
AMEN.

ADVENTURE

Flip to the adventures and ask the Holy Spirit what adventure He wants you to take today. After you take it, come back and fill this out. Have fun!

WHAT ADVENTURE DID YOU TAKE?

WHO DID JESUS ENCOUNTER?

Follow-up Info:

ACTIVATE LOVE ADVENTURE JOURNAL

THOUGHTS?

Fill this area with words/pictures from what happened and what you are learning.

OUR MISSION OUGHT TO BE JESUS'S MISSION — TO SEEK AND SAVE THAT WHICH IS LOST.

ACTIVATE LOVE ADVENTURE JOURNAL

LOVE THEM
ADVENTURES

THE ADVENTURE OF LOVING PEOPLE

We're carriers of God's love! We get the opportunity every day to share the love we have with those around us. We can do that in so many ways. I used to think that sharing Jesus with people meant that I needed to share the gospel with a perfectly scripted answer or see how many people I could pray for. Being a shy teenager, jumping right into something like that was so intimidating for me. I couldn't even pray in front of people, I was so fearful. I want you to know that loving people isn't complicated. It's actually simple. Your yes to love can simply be helping someone out at the grocery store, giving someone a sincere compliment, or saying "Jesus loves you" to the person who passes by. Many times a simple act of kindness can lead to conversation and connection with someone. Who knows what the Lord will do through your yes?

THE SMALL STEPS WILL BECOME BIG LEAPS.

Jesus is in you, and I believe your light will shine so brightly as you do these adventures. The small steps will become big leaps. I believe that as you go about the adventures in this book, you'll find yourself going from sharing a compliment to sharing the full gospel. If you're just beginning to take bold steps, you can start by doing more of the easier acts of kindness, but I want to encourage you to not stay there. Allow moments that stretch you to do the uncomfortable things, because in stretching there is extreme growth. As you continue to say yes, you'll find yourself in a place of being more fearless than fearful. In this book there are fifty-plus adventures you can go on. Pick whichever one (or more than one) you would like to go on each day. Remember, take the small steps and then challenge yourself to take the big leaps. You're not alone; the Holy Spirit wants to partner with you in this great adventure. You can do it. God is in you. You're courrageous! Have fun and go love people!

**TAKE A DEEP BREATH.
YOU'RE BRAVE.
THE HOLY SPIRIT
IS WITH YOU.**

ACTIVATE LOVE ADVENTURE JOURNAL

WHERE DO I START?

If you're wondering how to approach someone, here are a few things I find helpful.

TURN YOUR AFFECTION TOWARDS JESUS.

Give Jesus your attention and become aware of His presence around you. He is with you! Allow the Holy Spirit to be your guide. The Bible tells us that the Holy Spirit will teach us what to say (Luke 12:12). Be courageous; He is with you.

APPROACH AND INTRODUCE YOURSELF.

The first thing to do is approach the person the Lord has set on your heart. You can start out by saying hi and introducing yourself. Asking for their name makes people feel like you care. You can have a conversation with them or just get right to the reason why you approached them. I find that taking the time to talk with them makes people more open to hearing what you have to say about God.

WHAT DO I ACTUALLY SAY?

The Holy Spirit will give you the right things to say in the moment, as you lean in to Him. Thinking about who you're talking with helps when trying to figure out how to navigate conversation. I wouldn't talk to a child about God in the same way I would talk with an adult. I would share with them in a way that they would understand. As you go through this journey, stay open to what the Holy Spirit wants to do and allow Him to lead you through every adventure moment. Here are a few conversation starter ideas that you can keep in mind when approaching someone...

- "Do you have any pain in your body? I would love to pray for and bless you."

- "What brings you the most joy in life?" After they share, you can share the joy of knowing Jesus.

- "I'm practicing hearing the voice of God, and I felt led to come and share this word/picture. I feel in my heart that it's for you."

- "You know what I've found to be the greatest gift here on earth? To know the love of Jesus." Proceed by sharing the gospel with them.

- "I love your shirt/necklace/tattoo! What does it mean?" Find a way to bring Jesus into the middle of your conversation.

- "How are you doing today?" Through that question, find a way to encourage them and share the love of Jesus.

These are just a few of the many ways you can approach and start a conversation about the love of Jesus. Ultimately, just be you. The way you love someone won't look like the way your friend does. **YOUR PERSONALITY ROCKS!**

HERE ARE SOME HELPFUL TOOLS FOR YOUR JOURNEY...

YOU CAN DO IT.

It may be scary at first, but the more you do it, the more natural it becomes. You start to feel more excitement than fear.

KEEP YOUR MOTIVATIONS PURE.

You are not performing for God or man. Keep loving people out of a place of being so in love with Jesus that you can't help but share the love with others. It's not worth loving people out of a place feeling obligated. If you feel this way, focus your heart back on Jesus and the reason you love. We love because Jesus first loved us. Loving shouldn't ever feel like work; it should always be a joy.

LOVE NEVER FAILS.

If you ever feel like your encounter was awkward or something felt off, remember that the Lord delights in you and is so proud of your stepping out. When you do it out of love, failure is not in the picture.

COMMUNICATE WITH THE HOLY SPIRIT.

You're not alone. The Holy Spirit wants to partner with you. Try to keep a conversation with Him before, during, and after your encounter.

WALK IN OBEDIENCE IN THE BUSY TIMES TOO.

Often the Holy Spirit will ask us to love someone when we're in a rush to get somewhere or when our schedule seems so packed. It's so worth it to put down your own agenda and walk in His. A blessing awaits on the other side of that encounter.

DON'T COMPLICATE IT.

You don't need to strive. You get to adventure with Jesus, and all you need to do is rest in Him. Let His peace fill your heart and mind. Loving people feels like an obligation when you strive, but it's an exciting adventure when you take joy in Him.

TAKE RISKS.

Sometimes you'll feel compelled to do something super radical. If you feel Jesus leading you to it, then be brave and do it. He is with you! Isn't seeing someone encounter His love worth feeling a little awkward?

SHAKE THE DUST OFF YOUR FEET.

With stepping out and loving people, you will run into those who will reject you and not want to hear what you have to say. Don't get offended. Instead, shake the dust off your feet (see Matthew 10:14), thank the Lord for that moment, and then move on.

KEEP A POSTURE OF, "HERE I AM GOD".

Stay tuned throughout your day to see the Holy Spirit in how he's directing you. He's looking for those who are willing.

TAKE A FEW MINUTES TO PRACTICE WHAT IT WOULD LIKE FOR YOU TO APPROACH SOMEONE. YOU CAN EVEN DO THIS WITH A FRIEND.

Write out your conversation and ideas here...

*REMINDER: BE YOU.

LOVE PEOPLE IN SUCH A WAY THAT THOSE AROUND YOU **KNOW** THE JESUS IN YOU.

ACTIVATE LOVE ADVENTURE JOURNAL

BLOW THIS PAGE UP WITH COLOR.

With your bright colors, write something encouraging and then fold it up and leave this note in a book at the library or bookstore. It will be the best surprise!

ADVENTURE WITH SOME FRIENDS TODAY.

Go have fun shopping, and as you do that, find someone to pray for and share the love of Jesus with.

GO THROUGH THE  AND PAY FOR THE BILL OF THE PERSON BEHIND YOU, OR BLESS THE PERSON AT THE WINDOW.

Tape your receipt to this page...

A GATHERING PLACE FOR PRAYER

Find a prayer or worship set that you can go to, and spend time with Jesus. See if you can find someone there who you can encourage.

BAKE COOKIES FOR YOUR NEIGHBOR, OR BUY A YUMMY TREAT AT THE STORE FOR THEM.

ASK SOMEONE WHAT BRINGS THEM JOY. THEN SHARE THE REASON WHY YOU'RE SO FULL OF JOY.

*STARTING OFF WITH SIMPLE CONVERSATIONS LIKE THIS MAKE SHARING THE GOSPEL EASY.

ACTIVATE LOVE ADVENTURE JOURNAL

GIVE SOMEONE YOUR PARKING SPOT.

**THAT PARKING SPOT THAT YOU'RE EXCITED ABOUT TAKING...
TRY TO GIVE IT AWAY TO THE PERSON BEHIND YOU.**

FIND SOMEONE WORKING AND LET THEM KNOW WHAT A **GREAT JOB** THEY'RE DOING.

ACTIVATE LOVE ADVENTURE JOURNAL

FIND SOMEONE AT THE GAS STATION AND PAY FOR THEIR GAS.

✱AS YOU DO THIS, YOU CAN PRAY AND SHARE THE LOVE OF JESUS WITH THEM.

HAVE A CONVERSATION WITH A STRANGER TODAY.

In your conversation, find a way to encourage them and let them know that they're loved.

ACTIVATE LOVE ADVENTURE JOURNAL

SHOW YOUR NEIGHBOR KINDNESS.

DO A SMALL JOB FOR THEM OR FIND A WAY TO BE A <u>BLESSING</u> TO THEM.

GO UP TO SOMEONE AND ASK...

HOW CAN I BE PRAYING FOR YOU?

*IT CAN BE THAT SIMPLE. YOU CAN PRAY FOR THEM RIGHT THERE.

ACTIVATE LOVE ADVENTURE JOURNAL

GIVE SOMEONE A HUG.

This might seem strange, but sometimes people just need a hug. :)

GO TO YOUR LOCAL MALL
OR SHOPPING AREA AND
FIND SOMEONE TO
RADICALLY LOVE.

✗ ✗ ✗ ✗ ✗ ✗ ✗ ✗

ACTIVATE LOVE ADVENTURE JOURNAL

INVITE SOMEONE TO GET COFFEE OR LUNCH.

Pray with them, chat about Jesus, and remind them how extraordinary they are.

STOP SOMEONE IN A CROWDED AREA AND SHARE ABOUT HOW GOD KNOWS AND LOVES THEM.

HE SEES THE ONE!

ACTIVATE LOVE ADVENTURE JOURNAL

BRIGHTEN SOMEONE'S DAY.

Send someone a thoughtful card or gift.

✽FLOWERS CAN BE A FUN THING TO GIVE AWAY.

WHEREVER YOU GO TODAY...
MEET SOMEONE NEW.
ENCOURAGE & PRAY

ACTIVATE LOVE ADVENTURE JOURNAL

GIVE AWAY A BRAND-NEW
PAIR OF SHOES.
FIND SOMEONE TO LOVE AND BLESS.

SEND A THOUGHTFUL TEXT TODAY.

Ask the Holy Spirit for an encouraging word for that person.

ASK THE HOLY SPIRIT WHERE YOU SHOULD **GO TODAY.** WHEN SOMETHING COMES TO MIND, GO TO THAT PLACE AND LOVE SOMEONE THERE.

GO TO A BUS OR TRAIN STATION AND SHARE THE LOVE OF JESUS WITH SOMEONE THERE.

✽IF YOU END UP TAKING THE BUS OR TRAIN, TAPE YOUR TICKET TO THIS PAGE.

ACTIVATE LOVE ADVENTURE JOURNAL

SERVE YOUR COMMUNITY.

This can be done through picking up trash, volunteering at a local event, or finding an organization to work with. Go love the people of your community.

TAKE YOUR **STORY** THAT YOU WROTE DOWN AND GO SHARE IT WITH SOMEONE.

*TRY TO SHARE WITHIN 1-3 MINUTES.

ACTIVATE LOVE ADVENTURE JOURNAL

SHARE THE GOSPEL.

Take what you wrote down and go love someone with the greatest news.

BORROW YOUR FRIEND'S CAR AND GET IT CLEANED.

ACTIVATE LOVE ADVENTURE JOURNAL

IF IT'S A WARM DAY, GIVE AWAY A NEW PAIR OF SANDALS.

WRITE SOMETHING ENCOURAGING ON THIS PAPER.

Then tape it to the inside of your car.

ACTIVATE LOVE ADVENTURE JOURNAL

KEEP AN EYE OUT FOR SOMEONE WHO'S LOOKING SAD. :(

Ask the Lord how you can brighten their day.

FIND A GOVERNMENT OFFICE AND PRAY FOR SOMEONE THERE.

This might look like praying in your car or going inside a government building to find someone inside that you can love.

ACTIVATE LOVE ADVENTURE JOURNAL

TAKE A GROUP OF FRIENDS AND GO HAND OUT WATER BOTTLES (OR OTHER ESSENTIAL ITEMS) TO BLESS THOSE LIVING ON THE STREETS OR IN THE SHELTERS.

LEAVE A NOTE ON THE MIRROR IN THE PUBLIC BATHROOM. ↓

You can write it here, cut it out, and tape it to the mirror.

ACTIVATE LOVE ADVENTURE JOURNAL

GRAB THE TRASH THAT YOU SEE ON THE GROUND AND THROW IT AWAY.

FILL A BAG WITH GROCERIES.

Drop it off at someone's house and bless them.

*YOU CAN EVEN ADD AN ENCOURAGING NOTE WITH THE BAG.

ACTIVATE LOVE ADVENTURE JOURNAL

CUT THESE NOTES OUT AND LEAVE THEM PLACES, OR GIVE THEM AWAY.

YOU'RE VALUED & LOVED.
JESUS LOVES YOU!

JESUS CARES ABOUT YOU.
HE LOVES YOU!

YOU HAVE A PURPOSE.
JESUS LOVES YOU!

#ACTIVATE LOVE

#ACTIVATE LOVE

#ACTIVATE LOVE

LOVE SOMEONE AT SCHOOL OR AT WORK. DO AN UNEXPECTED KIND THING.

IF IT'S A COLD DAY, GIVE YOUR JACKET TO SOMEONE WHO NEEDS IT.

ACTIVATE LOVE ADVENTURE JOURNAL

GRAB STICKY NOTE.
WRITE ENCOURAGING NOTES AND LEAVE THEM ON PEOPLE'S BELONGINGS.

HOW CAN YOU BE A GODLY INFLUENCE ON SOCIAL MEDIA TODAY?

WHATEVER THAT CRAZY IDEA IS... GO FOR IT!

ACTIVATE LOVE ADVENTURE JOURNAL

ASK SOMEONE WHAT THEY'RE THANKFUL FOR. THEN SHARE WITH THEM WHY YOU'RE SO THANKFUL.

Fill this page with what you heard people say.

STAND BY
(OR CLOSE)
TO A
DISABLED
PARKING
SPOT, AND
WAIT THERE
UNTIL YOU
SEE SOMEONE
YOU CAN
PRAY FOR.

ACTIVATE LOVE ADVENTURE JOURNAL

BE A HAND FOR SOMEONE.

SHOW A PERSON KINDNESS BY OFFERING TO PICK UP GROCERIES OR BY DOING ANOTHER ODD JOB.

✽*THIS COULD ALSO BE ORGANIZING, CLEANING, RAKING, GARDENING, OR SOMETHING SIMILAR.*

GIVE A SINCERE COMPLIMENT TO SOMEONE.

ACTIVATE LOVE ADVENTURE JOURNAL

GIVE FLOWERS AWAY TO A STRANGER OR A FRIEND.

TIP YOUR WAITRESS EXTRA WELL.

Use your server's name and ask if you can pray for them.

ACTIVATE LOVE ADVENTURE JOURNAL

GO TO THE HOSPITAL OR FIND A MEDICINE AISLE.

Pray and love someone there.

FIND SOMEONE WHO'S HANGING OUT BY THEMSELVES. INTRODUCE YOURSELF AND INVITE THEM TO JOIN A GROUP ACTIVITY.

ACTIVATE LOVE ADVENTURE JOURNAL

SEND SOMEONE A THOUGHTFUL POSTCARD OR CARE PACKAGE. EVEN IF THEY'RE HALF WAY AROUND THE WORLD.

TAPE A
$5
BILL
TO THIS
PAGE.

*Come back toward the end and give it away!

ACTIVATE LOVE ADVENTURE JOURNAL

MAKE CARDS AND TAKE THEM TO A NURSING HOME.

VOICE MEMO SOMEONE IN YOUR CONTACTS.

You can love them by sharing any uplifting thing.

ACTIVATE LOVE ADVENTURE JOURNAL

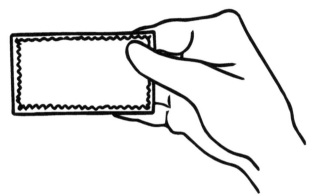

GRAB A BUSINESS CARD OFF THE WALL (OR JUST TAKE A PICTURE OF IT), AND CALL THAT PERSON UP AND LOVE THEM WITH ENCOURAGEMENT.

LET SOMEONE KNOW HOW MUCH <u>JESUS</u> LOVES THEM.

ACTIVATE LOVE ADVENTURE JOURNAL

UNEXPECTEDLY PAY FOR A STRANGER'S EXPENSE.

✽DOING THIS COULD LOOK LIKE TAKING SOMEONE OUT FOR LUNCH, BUYING THEM A GIFT, PAYING FOR SOMEONE'S GROCERIES, OR TAKING A FRIEND OUT FOR A FUN ADVENTURE.

WHAT WOULD YOU SAY TO YOUR GENERATION?

Write it out here and then copy this page and put it in three different locations.

ACTIVATE LOVE ADVENTURE JOURNAL

GO TO A COFFEE SHOP AND BUY THE PERSON BEHIND YOU A DRINK.

HOW DID THEY FEEL AFTER THAT?

GATHER YOUR <u>NEIGHBORS</u> TOGETHER AND DO AN OUTDOOR MOVIE NIGHT OR PICNIC.

ACTIVATE LOVE ADVENTURE JOURNAL

SHARE SOME OF YOUR STORY ON YOUR SOCIAL MEDIA ACCOUNT'S "STORY."

GO TO YOUR LOCAL LAUNDROMAT AND FIND SOMEONE TO PRAY FOR.

*You can even bless them with a load of laundry.

LOVE HIM

PART TWO

DAY SIXTEEN

I look to you, Father. You're my greatest desire. I am so thankful for your presence. All my attention is toward you. I give you this space and this time. Let your Spirit come and fill this room today. Thank you for being my Shepherd and leading me. I'm available for you. Come move and have your way. Take me on an adventure in your love! Amen.

TODAY I'M THANKFUL FOR...

SCRIPTURE I'M READING...

HIGHLIGHTS FROM THE WORD...

What is the Holy Spirit highlighting to me in Scripture, and what's on His heart about it?

ACTIVATE LOVE ADVENTURE JOURNAL

HOW I'M GOING TO APPLY WHAT I READ TODAY TO MY LIFE...

Write it out boldly here!

> "Call to me and I will answer you and I will tell you great and hidden things that you have not known."
> – JEREMIAH 33:3

LISTEN FOR HIS VOICE

Holy Spirit, what do you want to share with me today?

LEADING OF THE HOLY SPIRIT

Holy Spirit, what do you want to do through me today?

RESPOND
My prayer for today is...

▶ Based on your prayer today, make a declaration about yourself or something you're believing for. Declare it here! Feel free to tear it out and tape it somewhere. ▶

WORSHIP THE LORD IN A WAY THAT YOU NORMALLY DON'T.

GET <u>WILD</u> AND GET <u>UNCOMFORTABLE</u>.

ACTIVATE LOVE ADVENTURE JOURNAL

ADVENTURE

Flip to the adventures and ask the Holy Spirit what adventure He wants you to take today. After you take it, come back and fill this out. Have fun!

WHAT ADVENTURE DID YOU TAKE?

WHO DID JESUS ENCOUNTER?

Follow-up Info: 💬

THOUGHTS?

Fill this area with words/pictures from what happened and what you are learning.

DAY SEVENTEEN

I look to you, Father. You're my greatest desire. I am so thankful for your presence. All my attention is toward you. I give you this space and this time. Let your Spirit come and fill this room today. Thank you for being my Shepherd and leading me. I'm available for you. Come move and have your way. Take me on an adventure in your love! Amen.

TODAY I'M THANKFUL FOR...

SCRIPTURE I'M READING...

HIGHLIGHTS FROM THE WORD...

What is the Holy Spirit highlighting to me in Scripture, and what's on His heart about it?

ACTIVATE LOVE ADVENTURE JOURNAL

HOW I'M GOING TO APPLY WHAT I READ TODAY TO MY LIFE...
Write it out boldly here!

Silence the voice of fear, and let His voice
be what's heard in your ears.

LISTEN FOR HIS VOICE

Holy Spirit, what do you want to share with me today?

LEADING OF THE HOLY SPIRIT

Holy Spirit, what do you want to do through me today?

ACTIVATE LOVE ADVENTURE JOURNAL

RESPOND

My prayer for today is...

Based on your prayer today, make a declaration about yourself or something you're believing for. Declare it here! Feel free to tear it out and tape it somewhere.

AS YOU STEP OUT IN DAY-TO-DAY OBEDIENCE TO HIS LEADING, GOD WILL SHOW UP IN BIG WAYS.

LET HIM LEAD YOU

Those who belong to Christ Jesus have crucified the flesh with its passions and desires. Since we live by the Spirit, let us keep in step with the Spirit. – GALATIANS 5:24-25 ESV

What does a life being fearlessly led by the Holy Spirit look like? Being led by the Holy Spirit is exciting. Every day is an adventure with Him. Jesus sent the Holy Spirit to walk with us, guide us, and show His love through us. We have the opportunity to see the Holy Spirit working powerfully through our lives when we choose to surrender and lean into His plans.

SURRENDER

In 2018, I determined to grow in my responsiveness to the Holy Spirit's voice. I began to write down all the places that I felt He was leading me to go, and then I got in my car and started my journey. For three weeks, I drove across the United States and stepped out in courageous ways. One day, the map didn't work on my GPS, and I began to freak out. I felt the Holy Spirit say, "Brooke, I thought you wanted me to lead you." Immediately, I realized that I had trusted in my own ability to navigate rather than trusting in His ability to lead.

I kept driving, giving Him my fear of the unknown and surrendering my own plans to Him. The Holy Spirit gave me peace as I drove through the mountains. Around thirty minutes later, my GPS started working again. In that moment the Holy Spirit taught me that the key to living a life led by Him is releasing my own map and agenda and exchanging it for His. When we give our lives to Jesus, we are saying, "It is no longer I who live, but Christ lives in me" (Galatians 2:20 NKJV). God wants to take us on wild adventures with Him, but that requires we have a surrendered heart—a heart that invites the Lord to continually navigate our steps.

LEAN IN

Learning to be led by the Spirit also takes leaning in and not ignoring. To lean in means to live with openness and obedience to the Holy Spirit. When you hear the Holy Spirit speaking and prompting you to step out, that's an opportunity you have to lean in and say yes to the adventure. It's partnering with the Holy Spirit and choosing to trust Him, even when the instructions don't seem to make sense. It can be easy to say, "God, I'm available. Use my life for your glory." However, sometimes our cry to be used for His glory will be tested by our willingness to love someone when it's inconvenient. What will your response be when you're in a hurry, and He asks you to take time to love the person at the grocery store who looks lonely? He is with you. Don't let fear talk you out of that moment, but lean in to the voice of God and adventure with Him. It's so exciting to see people encounter God's love. As you step out in day-to-day obedience to His leading, God will show up in big ways. The adventures in this book are ideas, but ultimately the Holy Spirit is your guide. Ask the Holy Spirit to teach you to hear His voice and show you what it looks like to surrender and lean in.

LEAN IN TO THE HOLY SPIRIT TODAY, AND ASK HIM FOR THE NEXT PLACE HE WANTS TO TAKE YOU.

Write those places here, or draw a big red dot on that spot.

ADVENTURE

Flip to the adventures and ask the Holy Spirit what adventure He wants you to take today. After you take it, come back and fill this out. Have fun!

WHAT ADVENTURE DID YOU TAKE?

WHO DID JESUS ENCOUNTER?

Follow-up Info:

ACTIVATE LOVE ADVENTURE JOURNAL

THOUGHTS?

Fill this area with words/pictures from what happened and what you are learning.

DAY EIGHTEEN

I look to you, Father. You're my greatest desire. I am so thankful for your presence. All my attention is toward you. I give you this space and this time. Let your Spirit come and fill this room today. Thank you for being my Shepherd and leading me. I'm available for you. Come move and have your way. Take me on an adventure in your love! Amen.

TODAY I'M THANKFUL FOR...

SCRIPTURE I'M READING...

HIGHLIGHTS FROM THE WORD...

What is the Holy Spirit highlighting to me in Scripture, and what's on His heart about it?

HOW I'M GOING TO APPLY WHAT I READ TODAY TO MY LIFE...
Write it out boldly here!

IT'S SIMPLE, LEAN IN.

LISTEN FOR HIS VOICE

Holy Spirit, what do you want to share with me today?

LEADING OF THE HOLY SPIRIT

Holy Spirit, what do you want to do through me today?

RESPOND
My prayer for today is...

Based on your prayer today, make a declaration about yourself or something you're believing for. Declare it here! Feel free to tear it out and tape it somewhere.

WHAT DOES YOUR CONVERSATION WITH THE HOLY SPIRIT LOOK LIKE TODAY?

> **ME:**

> **GOD:**

> **ME:**

> **GOD:**

> **GOD:**

> **ME:**

ACTIVATE LOVE ADVENTURE JOURNAL

ADVENTURE

Flip to the adventures and ask the Holy Spirit what adventure He wants you to take today. After you take it, come back and fill this out. Have fun!

WHAT ADVENTURE DID YOU TAKE?

WHO DID JESUS ENCOUNTER?

Follow-up Info: 💬

THOUGHTS?

Fill this area with words/pictures from what happened and what you are learning.

DAY NINETEEN

I look to you, Father. You're my greatest desire. I am so thankful for your presence. All my attention is toward you. I give you this space and this time. Let your Spirit come and fill this room today. Thank you for being my Shepherd and leading me. I'm available for you. Come move and have your way. Take me on an adventure in your love! Amen.

TODAY I'M THANKFUL FOR...

SCRIPTURE I'M READING...

HIGHLIGHTS FROM THE WORD...

What is the Holy Spirit highlighting to me in Scripture, and what's on His heart about it?

ACTIVATE LOVE ADVENTURE JOURNAL

HOW I'M GOING TO APPLY WHAT I READ TODAY TO MY LIFE...

Write it out boldly here!

> "The Spirit gives life; the flesh counts for nothing. The words I have spoken to you—they are full of the Spirit and life."
> — JOHN 6:63

LISTEN FOR HIS VOICE

Holy Spirit, what do you want to share with me today?

LEADING OF THE HOLY SPIRIT

Holy Spirit, what do you want to do through me today?

RESPOND
My prayer for today is...

Based on your prayer today, make a declaration about yourself or something you're believing for. Declare it here! Feel free to tear it out and tape it somewhere.

EYES OF LOVE

"Let me ask you this. What would you do if you had one hundred sheep and one of them wandered off? Wouldn't you leave the ninety-nine on the hillside and go look for the one that had wondered away?" – MATTHEW 18:12 CEV

Within the primary job description of every believer is living a life that testifies about the Father, and seeing people through eyes of love. The love of Jesus that possesses our heart also needs to be what possesses our steps. Life can get busy. It's easy to get in the rhythm of going about our days as usual, but every day we have the opportunity to be sensitive to what the Holy Spirit is doing around us and lean in to divine moments (moments that are set up by Him).

The Holy Spirit is the best guide, and He wants to lead you into opportunities to love the person at the grocery store who's struggling with finances, the college girl thinking about suicide, or the person who has achieved so much yet feels empty inside. Millions of people are living every day full of brokenness, and many of them have never heard of the love of Jesus. We get to be the ones who see with eyes of love and express the love of Jesus to them.

SEEING THE ONE

Jesus loves touching people to manifest His love and glory. Some of my favorite moments are when the Holy Spirit leads me to share with someone in the midst of a busy, crowded area. I'll let them know how much Jesus loves them, and sometimes I'll share a few things that the Lord has told me about them. So many times they answer, "How did you know that?" or "It's crazy that you saw me in the midst of all these people and would come up to me." In those moments, I'm always so overwhelmed by the love of Jesus. God cares about people so much that He creates moments like this to display His love for them. He is the God who sees, and He wants to open our eyes to see people the way He does.

Open your eyes more and lean in to the Holy Spirit when He's prompting you to love someone. I believe that people will see the light and love of the Father as they look into your eyes. Jesus wants to use you today to be His hands and feet at the grocery store, at home with your family, at your job or at school, or in any environment you find yourself in partnership with the Holy Spirit, as you go throughout your day to love the one.

SEEING WHAT HE'S DOING

The Holy Spirit wants to communicate with us. Often when I'm at church or at the store, I'll say, "Holy Spirit, what are you doing in this place right now?" Most of the time I'll hear Him whisper something to my heart or highlight someone He wants to touch. Having this posture of heart says, "Jesus, I'm available to be your vessel." Doing this has really shifted things for me. I am less focused on myself and more aware of what He wants to do around me.

I want to challenge you to become more aware of what He's doing around you. Maybe He's asking you to approach someone, or maybe He's directing you to pray for a certain thing in the place you're at, or maybe He's leading you to go on one of the fun adventures in this book. Today, be open to what the Lord wants to do in and through you. The adventures He has for us are the best!

WHAT DOES IT LOOK LIKE FOR YOU TO SEE WITH <u>EYES OF LOVE?</u>

ACTIVATE LOVE ADVENTURE JOURNAL

FATHER,

I WANT EYES TO SEE PEOPLE THE WAY YOU SEE THEM. TEACH ME HOW TO LOVE THE WAY YOU DO. GIVE ME A HEART THAT IS CONSUMED WITH YOUR FIRE AND EYES THAT ARE CONSUMED WITH YOUR LOVE. I GIVE YOU MYSELF; LEAD MY STEPS AND GUARD MY WAY. FLOOD MY HEART WITH LOVE FOR THE LOST AND DIRECT ME TO THOSE YOU WANT TO BLESS THROUGH MY LIFE TODAY. THANK YOU, FATHER.

AMEN.

ADVENTURE

Flip to the adventures and ask the Holy Spirit what adventure He wants you to take today. After you take it, come back and fill this out. Have fun!

WHAT ADVENTURE DID YOU TAKE?

WHO DID JESUS ENCOUNTER?

Follow-up Info:

ACTIVATE LOVE ADVENTURE JOURNAL

THOUGHTS?

Fill this area with words/pictures from what happened and what you are learning.

DAY TWENTY

I look to you, Father. You're my greatest desire. I am so thankful for your presence. All my attention is toward you. I give you this space and this time. Let your Spirit come and fill this room today. Thank you for being my shepherd and leading me. I'm available for you. Come move and have your way. Take me on an adventure in your love! Amen.

TODAY I'M THANKFUL FOR...

SCRIPTURE I'M READING...

HIGHLIGHTS FROM THE WORD...

What is the Holy Spirit highlighting to me in Scripture, and what's on His heart about it?

HOW I'M GOING TO APPLY WHAT I READ TODAY TO MY LIFE...

Write it out boldly here!

He loves your voice. Your voice is mighty.
Let Him roar through you.

LISTEN FOR HIS VOICE

Holy Spirit, what do you want to share with me today?

LEADING OF THE HOLY SPIRIT

Holy Spirit, what do you want to do through me today?

RESPOND
My prayer for today is...

Based on your prayer today, make a declaration about yourself or something you're believing for. Declare it here! Feel free to tear it out and tape it somewhere.

YOU DON'T LACK. JESUS IS IN YOU, AND THAT MEANS YOU HAVE MORE THAN ENOUGH.

ACTIVATE LOVE ADVENTURE JOURNAL

WRITE THIS OUT TWENTY TIMES...
OR DO IT UNTIL IT SINKS DOWN INSIDE YOUR HEART.

JUST BECAUSE...

TIE SOMETHING THROUGH THIS PAGE!

ACTIVATE LOVE ADVENTURE JOURNAL

ADVENTURE

Flip to the adventures and ask the Holy Spirit what adventure He wants you to take today. After you take it, come back and fill this out. Have fun!

WHAT ADVENTURE DID YOU TAKE?

WHO DID JESUS ENCOUNTER?

Follow-up Info:

THOUGHTS?

Fill this area with words/pictures from what happened and what you are learning.

DAY TWENTY-ONE

I look to you, Father. You're my greatest desire. I am so thankful for your presence. All my attention is toward you. I give you this space and this time. Let your Spirit come and fill this room today. Thank you for being my Shepherd and leading me. I'm available for you. Come move and have your way. Take me on an adventure in your love! Amen.

TODAY I'M THANKFUL FOR...

SCRIPTURE I'M READING...

HIGHLIGHTS FROM THE WORD...

What is the Holy Spirit highlighting to me in Scripture, and what's on His heart about it?

ACTIVATE LOVE ADVENTURE JOURNAL

HOW I'M GOING TO APPLY WHAT I READ TODAY TO MY LIFE...
Write it out boldly here!

Keep tuning in to His frequency and listening in for His voice throughout your day. He loves sharing with you!

LISTEN FOR HIS VOICE

Holy Spirit, what do you want to share with me today?

LEADING OF THE HOLY SPIRIT

Holy Spirit, what do you want to do through me today?

RESPOND
My prayer for today is...

Based on your prayer today, make a declaration about yourself or something you're believing for. Declare it here! Feel free to tear it out and tape it somewhere.

THANK YOU, FATHER, FOR MY FAMILY. COME INVADE EVERY FAMILY MEMBER WITH YOUR ALL-CONSUMING LOVE. AWAKEN EVERY BROTHER, EVERY SISTER, EVERY PARENT, EVERY UNCLE, EVERY AUNT, EVERY GRANDPARENT, EVERY COUSIN, EVERY _____. CREATE A HUNGER IN MY FAMILY FOR THE WORD AND FOR YOUR PRESENCE. USE MY FAMILY TO TOUCH OUR NEIGHBORHOOD, OUR COMMUNITY, AND OUR NATION. AMEN.

FAMILY SET ABLAZE

Place me like a seal over your heart, like a seal on your arm; for love is as strong as death, its jealousy unyielding as the grave. It burns like blazing fire, like a mighty flame.
— SONG OF SONGS 8:6 ESV

God loves family. He doesn't want just daily encounters with individuals; He also wants to encounter entire families. What would happen if a whole family was set on fire for Jesus? What would soccer games, dance practice, and family gatherings look like? God loves your family. He wants your family to be saved and set on fire for Him.

A FAMILY THAT BELIEVES

God sees your family. He sees the members of your family who know Him, and He sees every person who doesn't have a relationship with Him yet. The desire of Jesus is that all would know Him. Let's believe today that any member of your family who isn't saved yet will come to know the wonderful love of Jesus. No matter what your family life looks like, if it's close or divided, God wants to restore and encounter each family member with His love.

You may look at your family and wonder, **How can God use my family to create impact?** Jesus doesn't need you to have an impeccable family line or a perfect family for Him to use you. He's looking for those who will just say yes to Him. The family line of Jesus included Rahab, a prostitute; David, an adulterer and murderer; and Jacob, a liar and deceiver; and it is through Jesus that we receive salvation. That's so powerful! He can use anyone with any family history. He wants to move through you and impact the world through your family. Through their faithfulness, your family can be the pioneers who mark a path of righteousness for future generations. Today, pray and believe that all of your family will encounter Jesus.

A FAMILY THAT BURNS

Jesus wants to use you to start a wildfire in your family, and He wants to use your family to start a wildfire in your home and in your community. Lean in to what it looks like as a family to seek the Lord and love people. Even if you're a youth or a young adult at home, or a single person living on your own, take some time to ask God what it looks like for you to love your family and create a home that hosts the presence of the Lord. This could be your demonstrating a daily lifestyle by the way you love, forgive, pray, or show kindness; as you do this, your family will see firsthand your relationship with God. One of my favorite quotes is from John Wesley: "I set myself on fire and people come and watch me burn." As you pray and as you burn, things can't stay the same. Soon you'll find the people around you are longing to burn with you.

Ask God to consume your family and saturate your day with more of Him. Your family gatherings, trips, grocery-store runs, and activities will look a whole lot different if you invite Him on the adventure with you. God wants to use your family in mighty ways!

WRITE OUT THE NAMES OF EACH INDIVIDUAL IN YOUR FAMILY WHO DOESN'T HAVE A RELATIONSHIP WITH GOD YET.

*Pray for them and ask the Lord for a word of encouragement regarding them. Share it with them when you feel the prompting of the Holy Spirit to do so.

GO AND SEEK THE LORD TODAY ON HIS VISION FOR YOUR IMMEDIATE FAMILY.

Then, at the end of the day, come back and write that vision plainly here.

ACTIVATE LOVE ADVENTURE JOURNAL

TAPE A PICTURE (OR DRAW ONE) OF YOUR FAMILY OR COMMUNITY TO THIS PAGE.

Let it be a reminder to daily be praying and believing for your family to encounter God.

ADVENTURE

Flip to the adventures and ask the Holy Spirit what adventure He wants you to take today. After you take it, come back and fill this out. Have fun!

WHAT ADVENTURE DID YOU TAKE?

WHO DID JESUS ENCOUNTER?

Follow-up Info:

ACTIVATE LOVE ADVENTURE JOURNAL

THOUGHTS?

Fill this area with words/pictures from what happened and what you are learning.

DAY TWENTY-TWO

I look to you, Father. You're my greatest desire. I am so thankful for your presence. All my attention is toward you. I give you this space and this time. Let your Spirit come and fill this room today. Thank you for being my Shepherd and leading me. I'm available for you. Come move and have your way. Take me on an adventure in your love! Amen.

TODAY I'M THANKFUL FOR...

SCRIPTURE I'M READING...

HIGHLIGHTS FROM THE WORD...

What is the Holy Spirit highlighting to me in Scripture, and what's on His heart about it?

HOW I'M GOING TO APPLY WHAT I READ TODAY TO MY LIFE...

Write it out boldly here!

> "The voice of the Lord is powerful;
> the voice of the Lord is majestic."
> — PSALM 29:4

LISTEN FOR HIS VOICE

Holy Spirit, what do you want to share with me today?

LEADING OF THE HOLY SPIRIT

Holy Spirit, what do you want to do through me today?

RESPOND
My prayer for today is...

Based on your prayer today, make a declaration about yourself or something you're believing for. Declare it here! Feel free to tear it out and tape it somewhere.

"YOU MAKE KNOWN TO ME THE PATH OF LIFE; YOU WILL **FILL ME WITH JOY** IN YOUR PRESENCE, WITH ETERNAL PLEASURES AT YOUR RIGHT HAND."

PSALM 16:11

WHAT IS JOY?
COLOR WHAT JOY IS TO YOU HERE.

ASK JESUS FOR MORE JOY TODAY!

FILL THIS PAGE WITH AS MANY SMILES AS YOU CAN! :)

ADVENTURE

Flip to the adventures and ask the Holy Spirit what adventure He wants you to take today. After you take it, come back and fill this out. Have fun!

WHAT ADVENTURE DID YOU TAKE?

WHO DID JESUS ENCOUNTER?

Follow-up Info: 💬

THOUGHTS?

Fill this area with words/pictures from what happened and what you are learning.

DAY TWENTY-THREE

I look to you, Father. You're my greatest desire. I am so thankful for your presence. All my attention is toward you. I give you this space and this time. Let your Spirit come and fill this room today. Thank you for being my Shepherd and leading me. I'm available for you. Come move and have your way. Take me on an adventure in your love! Amen.

TODAY I'M THANKFUL FOR...

SCRIPTURE I'M READING...

HIGHLIGHTS FROM THE WORD...

What is the Holy Spirit highlighting to me in Scripture, and what's on His heart about it?

HOW I'M GOING TO APPLY WHAT I READ TODAY TO MY LIFE...
Write it out boldly here!

> It is the glory of God to conceal a matter; to search out a matter is the glory of kings.
> — PSALM 29:4

LISTEN FOR HIS VOICE

Holy Spirit, what do you want to share with me today?

LEADING OF THE HOLY SPIRIT

Holy Spirit, what do you want to do through me today?

RESPOND
My prayer for today is...

Based on your prayer today, make a declaration about yourself or something you're believing for. Declare it here! Feel free to tear it out and tape it somewhere.

KINDNESS

Be kind and compassionate to one another, forgiving each other, just as in Christ God forgave you. – EPHESIANS 4:32

The expression of love is often seen through acts of kindness. Someone might not be able to receive what a believer has to say about Jesus, but when we show them love through doing something radically kind for them, they experience the love of Jesus in such a powerful way. I love how one act of kindness can create an amazing opportunity to share the gospel. Kindness may be just a seed, but remember that seeds soon become a harvest. Spread kindness like seeds and see what God will bring forth from it.

WHAT DOES KINGDOM KINDNESS LOOK LIKE?

The Bible says that kindness is one of the attributes of love. First Corinthians 13:4 tells us, **"Love is patient and kind"** (ESV). Kindness in Greek is **chrēsteuomai**, and it comes from the Greek word **chrēstos**, which means useful, serviceable, and good. The kindness of God working through you is more than your being kind; it's your activating and displaying love. Kindness is being useful and serving those around you. That may be simply helping a neighbor or giving someone your parking spot. It can be something small or something huge. Let Christ's kindness be seen in all that you do. As you go on your adventures today, remember that kindness is showing the love of the Father, and that one act of kindness can express a thousand words.

SHARING KINDNESS WHEN YOU DON'T FEEL LIKE IT

What if our reactions became a love transaction? We have an opportunity, when someone does us wrong, to show them the Father's forgiveness and love. We don't have to operate out of hate and frustration; instead, we can display the kindness of Jesus even to our enemies and those we don't agree with.

I've had times when someone really wronged me and I didn't want to love them at all, but then I would feel the Holy Spirit telling me to reach my hand out to them, forgive them, and love them. That can be hard, but that is what the Father did for us. He demonstrated His love even as we were sinners (Romans 5:8). We live in a day when many people don't know love like this. When you choose love transactions instead of quick, hateful reactions, it will shock the other person. If you want to look more like Jesus, then start looking like love.

Let's be the ones who build each other up. It's time to defeat hate with love. It's time to choose kindness over being right. It's time to love the people who think differently than we do, or who's values are not like ours. Let your light shine! Be quick to forgive and willing to go the extra mile. Ask the Lord for His thoughts about the person who wronged you, and get His perspective on frustrating situations. He will show you His heart as you lean in. Share His love with the world and spread His kindness like seeds.

WHAT DOES KINDNESS LOOK LIKE FOR YOU?

WRITE IT, DRAW IT, OR PAINT IT. HAVE FUN!

ACTIVATE LOVE ADVENTURE JOURNAL

WHO CAN YOU FORGIVE AND SHOW KINDNESS TO TODAY?

*IT MAY BE DIFFICULT TO LOVE THE PERSON WHO WRONGED YOU, BUT JESUS LOVES THAT PERSON AND WANTS TO DISPLAY HIS KINDNESS THROUGH YOU.

ADVENTURE

Flip to the adventures and ask the Holy Spirit what adventure He wants you to take today. After you take it, come back and fill this out. Have fun!

WHAT ADVENTURE DID YOU TAKE?

WHO DID JESUS ENCOUNTER?

Follow-up Info:

ACTIVATE LOVE ADVENTURE JOURNAL

THOUGHTS?

Fill this area with words/pictures from what happened and what you are learning.

DAY TWENTY-FOUR

I look to you, Father. You're my greatest desire. I am so thankful for your presence. All my attention is toward you. I give you this space and this time. Let your Spirit come and fill this room today. Thank you for being my Shepherd and leading me. I'm available for you. Come move and have your way. Take me on an adventure in your love! Amen.

TODAY I'M THANKFUL FOR...

SCRIPTURE I'M READING...

HIGHLIGHTS FROM THE WORD...

What is the Holy Spirit highlighting to me in Scripture, and what's on His heart about it?

ACTIVATE LOVE ADVENTURE JOURNAL

HOW I'M GOING TO APPLY WHAT I READ TODAY TO MY LIFE...

Write it out boldly here!

The voice of the Holy Spirit will mold you, shape you, teach you, convict you, lead you, and take you to wild places.

LISTEN FOR HIS VOICE

Holy Spirit, what do you want to share with me today?

LEADING OF THE HOLY SPIRIT

Holy Spirit, what do you want to do through me today?

RESPOND
My prayer for today is...

Based on your prayer today, make a declaration about yourself or something you're believing for. Declare it here! Feel free to tear it out and tape it somewhere.

GOD IS SO MUCH **BIGGER** THAN ANYTHING ELSE.

ACTIVATE LOVE ADVENTURE JOURNAL

REMEMBER WHAT GOD HAS DONE.

Write out all the victories that you have seen this year in your life. The big and small ones...

JUST BECAUSE...

TAKE THIS JOURNAL
SOMEWHERE
EXTRAORDINARY,
THEN CAPTURE THAT
HERE...

ACTIVATE LOVE ADVENTURE JOURNAL

ADVENTURE

Flip to the adventures and ask the Holy Spirit what adventure He wants you to take today. After you take it, come back and fill this out. Have fun!

WHAT ADVENTURE DID YOU TAKE?

WHO DID JESUS ENCOUNTER?

Follow-up Info: 💬

THOUGHTS?

Fill this area with words/pictures from what happened and what you are learning.

DAY TWENTY-FIVE

I look to you, Father. You're my greatest desire. I am so thankful for your presence. All my attention is toward you. I give you this space and this time. Let your Spirit come and fill this room today. Thank you for being my Shepherd and leading me. I'm available for you. Come move and have your way. Take me on an adventure in your love! Amen.

TODAY I'M THANKFUL FOR...

SCRIPTURE I'M READING...

HIGHLIGHTS FROM THE WORD...

What is the Holy Spirit highlighting to me in Scripture, and what's on His heart about it?

HOW I'M GOING TO APPLY WHAT I READ TODAY TO MY LIFE...
Write it out boldly here!

The Father delights in speaking to you. He wants to share His heart with you today.

LISTEN FOR HIS VOICE

Holy Spirit, what do you want to share with me today?

LEADING OF THE HOLY SPIRIT

Holy Spirit, what do you want to do through me today?

RESPOND
My prayer for today is...

Based on your prayer today, make a declaration about yourself or something you're believing for. Declare it here! Feel free to tear it out and tape it somewhere.

SOMETIMES THE HOLY SPIRIT WILL DIRECT US TO MINISTER TO SOMEONE IN THE <u>SIMPLEST</u> WAYS. HE USES THE THINGS WE THINK ARE <u>SIMPLE</u> TO MANIFEST HIS GLORY.

SIMPLE LOVE

I pray that out of his glorious riches he may strengthen you with power through his Spirit in your inner being, so that Christ may dwell in your hearts through faith. And I pray that you, being rooted and established in love, may have power, together with all the Lord's holy people, to grasp how wide and long and high and deep is the love of Christ. – EPHESIANS 3:16-18

The love of Jesus isn't complicated; really, it's simple. Every person on earth is so loved by Him. Sometimes we can get caught up in making things complicated, and that can stop us from following the Holy Spirit and stepping out to love people. More than once, I've talked myself out of opportunities to share the love of Jesus because I felt like I needed to know more or like I wouldn't be able to share accurately with someone of another lifestyle or religion. It's good to study the Bible and have knowledge of it, and the book of Proverbs talks about how important it is to get wisdom and understanding (4:5), but we can't let the feeling of not knowing enough stop us from simply loving someone in the way God created us to love. Be you! Your simple yes to love is so important and powerful.

SIMPLE YES

Living a lifestyle of love starts with willingness. The Holy Spirit wants to flow through you to touch those you come in contact with, but first you must surrender and say yes to what He wants to do through you. His presence doesn't leave you in those moments; He's always with you. When you said yes to Jesus, He came and dwelled within you. Every time you say yes to His Spirit leading, He will move through you. You don't have to know it all or be really outgoing; all Jesus is looking for is those who will simply say yes to Him. The best thing you can do is love the way God has created you to love. Simply say yes.

SIMPLE IS POWERFUL

Sometimes the Holy Spirit will direct us to minister to someone in the simplest ways. He uses the things we think are simple to manifest His glory. Many of the adventures in this book can seem small, but God can use each one in big ways.

One time, my husband and I pulled over and talked with someone on the side of the street who seemed like he was in need. We just talked with him. I offered prayer and a meal, but he didn't want either. He knew the Lord and even had a sign that said "Jesus loves you" on one side (the other side said "Homeless, please help"). We stayed for a few minutes, but never did anything else or gave anything to him (because he refused it); we simply talked to him and listened. As we were leaving, he told us twice how much it meant to him that we stopped. He was moved by our willingness to hang out and talk with him.

Never underestimate what seems so simple. Our kindness and love is seen by Jesus, and it's never in vain. We're sometimes the ones who plant the seeds and sometimes the ones who see the harvest. Trust the Lord that His Spirit is at work and He's going to do big things. Keep saying yes to Jesus, even in the simple things. Simple is powerful!

COLOR THE CORNER. COME BACK WHEN YOU NEED A REMINDER.

WHAT DOES IT LOOK LIKE FOR YOU TO DAILY SAY YES AND SIMPLY LOVE THE WAY YOU DO?

ADVENTURE

Flip to the adventures and ask the Holy Spirit what adventure He wants you to take today. After you take it, come back and fill this out. Have fun!

WHAT ADVENTURE DID YOU TAKE?

WHO DID JESUS ENCOUNTER?

Follow-up Info:

ACTIVATE LOVE ADVENTURE JOURNAL

THOUGHTS?

Fill this area with words/pictures from what happened and what you are learning.

DAY TWENTY-SIX

I look to you, Father. You're my greatest desire. I am so thankful for your presence. All my attention is toward you. I give you this space and this time. Let your Spirit come and fill this room today. Thank you for being my Shepherd and leading me. I'm available for you. Come move and have your way. Take me on an adventure in your love! Amen.

TODAY I'M THANKFUL FOR...

SCRIPTURE I'M READING...

HIGHLIGHTS FROM THE WORD...

What is the Holy Spirit highlighting to me in Scripture, and what's on His heart about it?

ACTIVATE LOVE ADVENTURE JOURNAL

HOW I'M GOING TO APPLY WHAT I READ TODAY TO MY LIFE...
Write it out boldly here!

"The Spirit of the Lord will rest on him — the Spirit of wisdom and of understanding, the Spirit of counsel and of might, the Spirit of the knowledge and fear of the Lord."
— ISAIAH 11:2

LISTEN FOR HIS VOICE

Holy Spirit, what do you want to share with me today?

LEADING OF THE HOLY SPIRIT

Holy Spirit, what do you want to do through me today?

RESPOND
My prayer for today is...

Based on your prayer today, make a declaration about yourself or something you're believing for. Declare it here! Feel free to tear it out and tape it somewhere.

WHO IN LEADERSHIP CAN YOU BE PRAYING FOR THIS WEEK?

1.

2.

3.

ACTIVATE LOVE ADVENTURE JOURNAL

ADVENTURE

Flip to the adventures and ask the Holy Spirit what adventure He wants you to take today. After you take it, come back and fill this out. Have fun!

WHAT ADVENTURE DID YOU TAKE?

WHO DID JESUS ENCOUNTER?

Follow-up Info:

THOUGHTS?

Fill this area with words/pictures from what happened and what you are learning.

DAY TWENTY-SEVEN

I look to you, Father. You're my greatest desire. I am so thankful for your presence. All my attention is toward you. I give you this space and this time. Let your Spirit come and fill this room today. Thank you for being my Shepherd and leading me. I'm available for you. Come move and have your way. Take me on an adventure in your love! Amen.

TODAY I'M THANKFUL FOR...

SCRIPTURE I'M READING...

HIGHLIGHTS FROM THE WORD...

What is the Holy Spirit highlighting to me in Scripture, and what's on His heart about it?

HOW I'M GOING TO APPLY WHAT I READ TODAY TO MY LIFE...

Write it out boldly here!

> "Ask and it will be given to you; seek and you will find; knock and the door will be opened to you."
> — MATTHEW 7:7

LISTEN FOR HIS VOICE

Holy Spirit, what do you want to share with me today?

LEADING OF THE HOLY SPIRIT

Holy Spirit, what do you want to do through me today?

RESPOND
My prayer for today is...

Based on your prayer today, make a declaration about yourself or something you're believing for. Declare it here! Feel free to tear it out and tape it somewhere.

TAKE **5** MINUTES TODAY TO PRAY FOR YOUR NATION AND **5** MINUTES TO PRAY FOR ANOTHER NATION THAT THE LORD SETS ON YOUR HEART. OR YOU CAN <u>CHOOSE</u> TO DO IT LONGER.

You can also do a prayer walk in your neighborhood and declare things over your community.

MAKING HIM KNOWN

"Declare his glory among the nations, his marvelous deeds among all peoples." – 1 CHRONICLES 16:24

Make the name of Jesus known! As believers we're called to not stay silent, but to make His name known to the world and share the hope we have with others. We're called to be unashamed of the name of Jesus.

I once told a lady next to me on a plane that Jesus loves her, and she responded that she doesn't believe in being vocal about her faith, which is why she's more reserved with it. I told her that when I love someone so much, I can't help but talk about them. We're called to boldly proclaim Jesus's love to those in our community and nation. We can't stay silent and let the rocks cry out (see Luke 19:40). Let's be ones who carry the love of Jesus and make His name famous throughout the world.

MAKING HIM KNOWN IN YOUR COMMUNITY

No matter how dark a community is or how far its people are from the truth, the light of Jesus will always be greater. You carry the light of Jesus, and He wants to shine through you to touch your neighborhood and your community. You were made to be an imitator of Christ and to shine forth His glory in the earth.

We pass by broken and sad people every day. What if a community was awakened because of a few lovers of Jesus who decided to smile and shine everywhere they went. God is looking for those who will say yes and who will dare to share their love with the people around them. You were created for such a time as this. You are in a place—at school, at a job, etc.—that many others are not. You have the opportunity to be an influence right where you are. God wants to overflow through your life. Pray for an awakening and a movement in your community. Believe that His kingdom will come in your school, workplace, and neighborhood. Let's not just want to see movement happen; let's be the movement.

MAKING HIM KNOWN IN YOUR NATION

Jesus told us to go into all the world and declare His name and make disciples (Matthew 28:19). He loves every tribe and every nation, and He longs for all to know Him. If right now, "nation" means going to a new country, praying for a nation, encouraging others from across the globe by mail or media platforms, or showing kindness and love to someone who represents another nation, you were created to reach and love all who cross your path. Not only does God want to use your life to affect the nations of the world, but He also wants to overflow through you to bring impact to your own nation. Ask God what that looks like. Pray for your leaders and pray that all would come to know the most powerful and most glorious name of Jesus. Let's make the name of Jesus known in our nation and in the nations of the earth.

HOW CAN
YOU BE A
VOICE OR
INFLUENCE
IN YOUR
COMMUNITY?

"OUR FATHER IN HEAVEN,
HALLOWED BE YOUR NAME,
YOUR KINGDOM COME,
YOUR WILL BE DONE, ON EARTH
(IN)_____
_{write where you live.}
AS IT IS IN HEAVEN."

MATTHEW 6:9-10

DRAW YOUR CITY SKYLINE OR TAKE A PICTURE OF IT AND TAPE IT HERE!

ADVENTURE

Flip to the adventures and ask the Holy Spirit what adventure He wants you to take today. After you take it, come back and fill this out. Have fun!

WHAT ADVENTURE DID YOU TAKE?

WHO DID JESUS ENCOUNTER?

Follow-up Info:

ACTIVATE LOVE ADVENTURE JOURNAL

THOUGHTS?

Fill this area with words/pictures from what happened and what you are learning.

DAY TWENTY-EIGHT

I look to you, Father. You're my greatest desire. I am so thankful for your presence. All my attention is toward you. I give you this space and this time. Let your Spirit come and fill this room today. Thank you for being my Shepherd and leading me. I'm available for you. Come move and have your way. Take me on an adventure in your love! Amen.

TODAY I'M THANKFUL FOR...

SCRIPTURE I'M READING...

HIGHLIGHTS FROM THE WORD...

What is the Holy Spirit highlighting to me in Scripture, and what's on His heart about it?

HOW I'M GOING TO APPLY WHAT I READ TODAY TO MY LIFE...
Write it out boldly here!

The Holy Spirit speaks with power and authority. What He says will line up with Scripture, and His voice is never condemning or fear-instilling. He speaks life-giving truth.

LISTEN FOR HIS VOICE

Holy Spirit, what do you want to share with me today?

LEADING OF THE HOLY SPIRIT

Holy Spirit, what do you want to do through me today?

RESPOND

My prayer for today is...

Based on your prayer today, make a declaration about yourself or something you're believing for. Declare it here! Feel free to tear it out and tape it somewhere.

WHAT IS THE MOST <u>RADICAL</u> THING YOU'VE EVER DONE FOR JESUS?

*WHAT IF YOU DID IT AGAIN?

ACTIVATE LOVE ADVENTURE JOURNAL

THE RIGHTEOUS ARE AS BOLD AS A LION.

PROVERBS 28:1

HE MADE YOU BRAVE AND BOLD.

JUST BECAUSE...

DRAW REALLY **BOLD** LINES!

ACTIVATE LOVE ADVENTURE JOURNAL

ADVENTURE

Flip to the adventures and ask the Holy Spirit what adventure He wants you to take today. After you take it, come back and fill this out. Have fun!

WHAT ADVENTURE DID YOU TAKE?

WHO DID JESUS ENCOUNTER?

Follow-up Info: 💬

THOUGHTS?

Fill this area with words/pictures from what happened and what you are learning.

DAY TWENTY-NINE

I look to you, Father. You're my greatest desire. I am so thankful for your presence. All my attention is toward you. I give you this space and this time. Let your Spirit come and fill this room today. Thank you for being my Shepherd and leading me. I'm available for you. Come move and have your way. Take me on an adventure in your love! Amen.

TODAY I'M THANKFUL FOR...

SCRIPTURE I'M READING...

HIGHLIGHTS FROM THE WORD...

What is the Holy Spirit highlighting to me in Scripture, and what's on His heart about it?

HOW I'M GOING TO APPLY WHAT I READ TODAY TO MY LIFE...
Write it out boldly here!

Ask the Holy Spirit to renew your mind and purify your heart.
Let your mind become like a blank canvas, and then
let His words paint a beautiful picture upon it.

LISTEN FOR HIS VOICE

Holy Spirit, what do you want to share with me today?

LEADING OF THE HOLY SPIRIT

Holy Spirit, what do you want to do through me today?

RESPOND

My prayer for today is...

Based on your prayer today, make a declaration about yourself or something you're believing for. Declare it here! Feel free to tear it out and tape it somewhere.

IT'S ALL ABOUT IT HIM.

Let your flesh die. What areas in your life need to be fully surrendered to Him?

ACTIVATE LOVE ADVENTURE JOURNAL

ONLY HIM

When you abide under the shadow of Shaddai, you are hidden in the strength of God Most High. – PSALM 91:1 TPT

It's all about Jesus. Life isn't about seeking our own glory; we're called to bring Him glory in all that we do. He calls us to walk in purity and stay hidden in Him. Being hidden in Him means not seeking to be publicly acknowledged, but striving to make Him known and build His kingdom on earth. It's all about Jesus, and all the glory belongs to Him.

STAYING HIDDEN

Hide yourself in the Father. This doesn't mean hiding yourself from people. It's simply finding your safety and satisfaction in the Father and not in man or in performance. It's keeping your eyes fixed on Jesus and not on yourself. It's about abiding in His shadow and not trying to cast your own shadow.

When you start making your life about the followers and the likes, or you start boasting about what you've accomplished, you'll find yourself drifting further from the main purpose. Jesus is our main purpose, and our hearts need to stay hidden in that. We cannot operate without Him. Performance is filled with selfishness and pride. Keep your heart pure and open. God blesses the pure in heart (Matthew 5:8). Purity is powerful; the presence of Jesus rests on the things that are pure. Today, ask the Holy Spirit to wash your heart of any selfish or impure motives. The Lord delights in you and wants to impact the world through your life. When something incredible happens, never forget who the glory and honor belong to. Always point people back to the Father. As you go on adventures today, remember that this isn't a performance; it's about King Jesus. It's about loving people in such a way that those around you see the Jesus in you.

BUILDING HIS KINGDOM

We're called to go and make disciples, and to build the family and kingdom of God. You play an important part on this earth. Jesus loves you so much and wants to use your life to display His love everywhere you go.

We aren't here to build without Him. We see how that went in the story of the Tower of Babel (Genesis 11). Building on our own will leave us scattered and without true legacy. We're to build His kingdom. No matter what you do, ask Jesus to be King in it. It's all about Him! It's so much better with the favor and blessing of Jesus on it. We get to build His kingdom in our daily lives, activities, and adventures of loving people.

"ONE THING I ASK FROM THE LORD, **THIS ONLY DO I SEEK:** THAT I MAY DWELL IN THE HOUSE OF THE LORD ALL THE DAYS OF MY LIFE, TO GAZE ON THE BEAUTY OF THE LORD AND TO SEEK HIM IN HIS TEMPLE."

PSALM 27:4

FATHER,

KEEP ME HIDDEN IN YOU. TAKE ME DEEPER IN MY RELATIONSHIP WITH YOU. SHOW ME WHAT IT LOOKS LIKE TO PASSIONATELY PURSUE YOU ALL THE DAYS OF MY LIFE. THANK YOU FOR THE OPPORTUNITIES YOU HAVE GIVEN ME TODAY. SHOW ME WHAT IT LOOKS LIKE TO LOVE YOU IN ALL THAT I SAY AND DO. I WANT TO SEE YOUR FAMILY GROW, SO I ASK FOR YOUR THOUGHTS AND IDEAS ON HOW I CAN LOVE THE PEOPLE AROUND ME. I GIVE YOU ALL THE GLORY FOR EVERY MOMENT IN THESE LAST THIRTY DAYS. I SAY YES TO ALL THE MANY MORE ADVENTURES WITH YOU.

AMEN.

JUST BECAUSE...

STAR GAZE
THINK ABOUT THE WONDER OF IT ALL.

ADVENTURE

Flip to the adventures and ask the Holy Spirit what adventure He wants you to take today. After you take it, come back and fill this out. Have fun!

WHAT ADVENTURE DID YOU TAKE?

WHO DID JESUS ENCOUNTER?

Follow-up Info:

ACTIVATE LOVE ADVENTURE JOURNAL

THOUGHTS?

Fill this area with words/pictures from what happened and what you are learning.

DAY THIRTY

I look to you, Father. You're my greatest desire. I am so thankful for your presence. All my attention is toward you. I give you this space and this time. Let your Spirit come and fill this room today. Thank you for being my Shepherd and leading me. I'm available for you. Come move and have your way. Take me on an adventure in your love! Amen.

TODAY I'M THANKFUL FOR...

SCRIPTURE I'M READING...

HIGHLIGHTS FROM THE WORD...

What is the Holy Spirit highlighting to me in Scripture, and what's on His heart about it?

HOW I'M GOING TO APPLY WHAT I READ TODAY TO MY LIFE...
Write it out boldly here!

Lean back on Jesus's chest and feel His heartbeat for you.

LISTEN FOR HIS VOICE

Holy Spirit, what do you want to share with me today?

LEADING OF THE HOLY SPIRIT

Holy Spirit, what do you want to do through me today?

RESPOND
My prayer for today is...

Based on your prayer today, make a declaration about yourself or something you're believing for. Declare it here! Feel free to tear it out and tape it somewhere.

WHAT WAS YOUR FAVORITE MOMENT THROUGH THIS ADVENTURE?

Write it out here!

ADVENTURE

Flip to the adventures and ask the Holy Spirit what adventure He wants you to take today. After you take it, come back and fill this out. Have fun!

WHAT ADVENTURE DID YOU TAKE?

WHO DID JESUS ENCOUNTER?

Follow-up Info:

THOUGHTS?

Fill this area with words/pictures from what happened and what you are learning.

YOU'RE BRAVE.

YOU MADE IT TO THE END OF THIS JOURNAL, BUT IT'S ONLY THE BEGINNING OF SOMETHING EXTRAORDINARY. KEEP THE ADVENTURE GOING.

ACTIVATE LOVE ADVENTURE JOURNAL

OVERFLOW

CONTINUING A LIFE OF OVERFLOW AFTER THE 30-DAY ADVENTURE

KEEP THE LOVE GOING!

The adventure isn't just a 30-day thing or a one-time divine encounter. It's a lifestyle! We're called to be people who overflow every day with His love. We do this by (1) staying connected to Jesus, (2) pouring into and discipling those God has placed in our lives, and (3) continuing to choose every day to love people. Let's not just say we will do this or even just think about it; let's make a plan on how we will be ones who daily walk this out.

YOUR EVERYDAY YES WILL CREATE AN OVERFLOW THAT WILL IMPACT THE PEOPLE AROUND YOU.

STAYING CONNECTED

You were created to know God every single day. Connection with Him is everything. Above all else that you take from this book, this is the number one thing that I would love to sink deep into your heart.

JESUS LONGS TO FLOW THROUGH YOU, BUT HE WANTS TO FIRST FILL YOU.

We're called to love Him first and people second. I've seen people mix this up (even myself at times), and it's left them empty and doing ministry with just noise and no connection. This is so dangerous. He wants to awaken love in you and show His love through you. We cannot run on empty; we need Him. He is our source.

COME TO THE WATERS AND DRINK IN HIS LOVE (SEE ISAIAH 55:1). TASTE AND SEE THAT THE LORD IS GOOD AND THAT HIS LOVE FOR YOU IS IMMENSE. JESUS LONGS FOR CONTINUAL CONNECTION WITH YOU!

WHAT DOES CONNECTION LOOK LIKE FOR YOU?

Write it here!

DON'T RUN ON EMPTY;
GET IN HIS PRESENCE.
LET HIM FILL YOU WITH
HIS LOVE.

ACTIVATE LOVE ADVENTURE JOURNAL

DISCIPLING OTHERS

"GO THEREFORE AND MAKE DISCIPLES OF ALL NATIONS, BAPTIZING THEM IN THE NAME OF THE FATHER AND OF THE SON AND OF THE HOLY SPIRIT." - MATTHEW 28:19 ESV

We are called to make disciples. I think many times we can go from encounter to encounter and forget to make it a priority to see people grow in Jesus. All moments with people won't be the same. Some of the love adventures you go on may just be one-time moments with that person, but I want to challenge and encourage you to ask the Holy Spirit to guide you, in those adventure moments, to whomever He would like you to follow up with.

DISCIPLESHIP TAKES A LIFE-CHANGING MOMENT TO A LIFE-CHANGED PERSON.

Take some time to help someone get connected, learn, and discover more about God. Become a friend to them. Today, pray and ask the Holy Spirit to show you ways that you can help someone along this great adventure of knowing Jesus and loving people.

*REMINDER: YOU DON'T HAVE TO KNOW IT ALL TO HELP SOMEONE; ALL YOU HAVE TO DO IS KNOW HIM.

FOLLOW-UP:

Write down the names of three people God sets on your heart who you can help disciple and encourage right now.

1 NAME: _____

📱 _____

📷 _____

HANGOUT LOCATION:

2 NAME: _____

📱 _____

📷 _____

HANGOUT LOCATION:

3 NAME: _____

📱 _____

📷 _____

HANGOUT LOCATION:

ACTIVATE LOVE ADVENTURE JOURNAL

FIND A BIBLE TO GIVE AWAY TO ONE OF THE PEOPLE ON YOUR FOLLOW-UP LIST.

TO WHAT CHURCHES OR GROUPS IN YOUR AREA CAN YOU POINT NEW BELIEVERS?

INVITE A FRIEND TO GO ON AN ADVENTURE WITH YOU.

Encourage them that they can be brave too.

LIFESTYLE OF LOVE

You get to make a decision now. Will you put this book on a shelf, forget about the adventure, and get too busy to love, or will you choose to hide every revelation and moment from this adventure in your heart and continue to walk boldly in love?

THIS ADVENTURE TAKES AN EVERYDAY <u>YES</u>.

In my life, I've seen the passion to love become dim at times, simply because I either got "too busy" to love or I slipped back into fear of man. Keep saying yes to Jesus and loving people even when you don't feel like it. Being obedient to Jesus can be uncomfortable, inconvenient, and scary, but I promise you it will always be rewarding. Learning how to ride a bike isn't easy, but once you get the hang of it, it becomes natural. Same thing with loving people; the more you step out, the more it will feel like an everyday normal thing.

Say yes to His voice and yes to the moments He's given to you. God wants to use you to bring light to your city, hope to the people on the streets, freedom for that friend that feels stuck and alone, and love to that person in front of you at the store. Don't wait for when you "think" it's a better time; there's no better time than right now. This is the time to be brave and to walk in bold love.

MAY THE GOD OF HOPE **FILL** YOU WITH ALL JOY AND PEACE AS YOU TRUST IN HIM, SO THAT YOU MAY **OVERFLOW** WITH HOPE BY THE POWER OF THE HOLY SPIRIT.

ROMANS 15:13

*REMEMBER, THE KEY IS TO BE FILLED SO THAT YOU CAN OVERFLOW.

HOW DO YOU WANT TO LIVE AN OVERFLOWING LIFESTYLE OF LOVE EVERY DAY?

Write out your declaration here and go live it out there.

*FEEL FREE TO TEAR THIS PAGE OUT AND PUT IT SOMEWHERE WHERE YOU CAN BE REMINDED OF THIS DAILY.

ACTIVATE LOVE ADVENTURE JOURNAL

LET ME LEAVE YOU WITH A FEW REMINDERS:

Love Him first and then love people.

Always stay open to the Holy Spirit.

Jesus is with you.

You were created to love.

If you get rejected, shake it off and keep going.

You have resurrection power inside you.

Stay aware of what He's doing in your everyday life.

Love Him with all your heart.

You're His child;

live every day knowing that.

BE LOVE.
ONE YES WILL LEAD TO MORE.

ACTIVATE LOVE ADVENTURE JOURNAL

ACKNOWLEDGMENTS

I am so thankful to be surrounded by a community and family who love me. Their love has molded me into who I am today. For years, I was so timid and afraid of adventures like those found in **Activate Love**, but my family and friends have inspired me to live courageously. I am forever thankful for them!

THERE ARE SO MANY TO NAME, BUT HERE ARE JUST A FEW...

JESUS:

My everything. This adventure is all about YOU. I am able to love because you first loved me. The day that I felt you prompting me to go to my computer to write, it honestly freaked me out, but my life is forever changed because of it. You have given me a greater love and compassion for the world. You're my hero! I give you all the glory!

JONATHAN:

You're my knight in shining armor. You're the greatest husband that I could ever ask for. I would still be writing this book if it wasn't for you. Thank you for constantly encouraging, caring for, and loving me. You're a man that takes action and gives Jesus your bold yes. I am so grateful I get to call you my husband! Love you!

GRANDMA LINDA:

The most incredible artist I know. Thank you for taking time to draw a few of the illustrations in this book. My sweet grandma, you're beyond gifted! I'm inspired by your prayer life and your constant love for your family. Thank you, Grandma, for being amazing!

MY FAMILY:

Wow, I am grateful for every one of you! You all love people in crazy ways. Ever since I was a young girl, each of you has shown me what love looks like. Thank you, Mom, for showing me love through the way you pray and take care of your children. Thank you, Dad, for always providing and stopping in the store for this one. Thank you, siblings, grandparents, aunts, and uncles, for showing love through giving your time, finances, and resources. I am so thankful for each one of you!

CAMBY DESIGNS:

Thank you, Aaron and the Camby team! This book has really come to life with the illustrations and layout that you implemented. Your team does things with integrity, excellence, and passion for the vision. I'm so thankful to have had the opportunity to work alongside you!

ABOUT THE AUTHOR

Brookelynn Landis is passionate about making the name of Jesus famous throughout the earth and seeing people encounter the love of the Father. Loving Jesus is her favorite thing to do. She's realized how important it is to not just show the world kindness and love, but to live a life that seeks the presence of Jesus. Her desire is to see people continually pursuing the heart of God and daily living out what it looks like to be a follower of Jesus.

Brookelynn grew up in Wisconsin with her seven siblings and her loving parents. At the age of seventeen, God called her to move to Texas, where she spent four years ministering with a Christian dance company. It was there that God stirred in her heart to gather friends to love people in downtown Dallas. In doing so, she realized how simple it is to love someone and how complicated sometimes we make it. Her desire is for people to see how easy and simple loving others can be.

Brookelynn is married to Jonathan, the man of her dreams. Together they're pursuing the Lord and allowing His love to mold every part of their marriage, businesses, and endeavors. They love traveling and spreading the good news.

Lightning Source UK Ltd.
Milton Keynes UK
UKHW021518040422
401067UK00009B/1572